DAKOTA TERRITORY

A Tap Duncan Western

DAKOTA TERRITORY

A Tap Duncan Western

by

Brad Prowse

THIS NOVEL HAS BEEN COMPARED TO SHANE,
HONDO, THE SEARCHERS, THE VIRGINIAN...
ALWAYS UNFAVORABLY.

ISBN: 1-58721-419-9

1stBooks – rev. 6/7/00

ABOUT THE BOOK

It is 1875, the last year the Sioux will spend as a free people. Pressure from settlers, gold seekers and the Army will soon bring a crisis to the Plains Indian's way of life. Added to this volatile mix are gunrunners. They provide the horse Indians with a weapon in many ways superior to what the Army has, increasing their ability and desire to make war.

Colonel Bruster, commandant of Fort McPherson in Dakota Territory, calls his old friend, Tap Duncan--sometimes lawman, sometimes Army scout--into this mix. Bruster hopes Tap might be able to stop the gunrunning and remove one element of heat from the powder keg he feels the territory sits upon.

Tap arrives at McPherson but finds his job complicated by Buffalo Lance, a Sioux who feels he has good reason to kill Tap, Bruster's daughter, Matty, a love from earlier times, her suitor, Captain Hawthorne, who likes Tap about as much as Buffalo Lance does, and the gunrunners themselves. Tap will be busy just keeping alive.

PROLOGUE

In 1867, several bands of Sioux signed an agreement with the United States Government--the Red Cloud Treaty--that led to the abandonment of three frontier forts and a promise by the army to keep whites out of Sioux Territory. Seemingly, the 'Indian Problem' had been resolved.

However, with the Nation's centennial nearing, there was constant pressure on Washington from settlers and gold seekers to scrap the Red Cloud Treaty. The malaise from the Panic of 1873 still held the country's economy in bondage and many Americans--white Americans--wanted to open up more land for settlement, land that had been promised to the Indians. Using the army, Washington 'encouraged' the tribes to retire to reservations instead of continuing their nomadic wanderings in search of the buffalo.

The Indians, naturally, chafed at the destruction of their former way of life. They wanted the Great White Father to live up to the stipulations of the Red Cloud Treaty--to keep whites out of the Black Hills and allow them to leave their reservations to hunt. In reality, after Custer's Expedition in 1874 discovered gold in the sacred Black Hills, the fate of the Sioux was sealed. 1875 would be the last year the Plains Tribes would enjoy as a free people.

Adding fuel to this explosive situation were men who supplied repeating rifles and ammunition to the tribes. This was particularly prevalent in the eastern portion of Dakota Territory, near the vicinity of Forts Lincoln, Rice and, particularly, McPherson. Colonel Bruster, commander of Fort McPherson, finally sent to Fort Rice for Tap Duncan, an old friend from the War and a top scout and former lawman. Colonel Bruster hoped that Tap could ferret out whoever was supplying the tribes with repeating arms. If possible, Tap might also meet with the tribes that were presently out hunting buffalo and try to defuse the tension that was running high between the Indians and whites.

Tap had only been at Fort McPherson for two weeks when he suddenly found himself in far closer contact to both the Sioux and their firearms than he cared to...

1

The flap of hide flew back and Buffalo Lance stepped out of the tipi. He was a short man, broad through the chest, with thick, sinewy arms. He wore only a breechclout. The black and vermilion paint that covered his face and upper body glistened its freshness in the light flickering from the nearby council fire a half-dozen yards away. Around the fire the tribe's important men sat in a semi-circle. But it was the white man, tethered to a post set upright in the ground not far from the fire, that occupied Buffalo Lance's attention.

"Buffalo Lance!" the white man called, sitting wearily in the dirt at the base of the pole. "My brother..." he started to say, but the Indian cut him short.

"You are a liar, Many Speaks!" Buffalo Lance shouted, striding past the council fire that kept the dark at bay beyond the nearest tipis. He stopped at the post and looked down at the white man sitting there, looming over him like some bird of prey. "You are not my brother!" Buffalo Lance, said, spitting out his words, his face hard, his eyes gleaming like pieces of flint in the reflection of the fire. "You talk with two faces!"

Tap Duncan gripped the pole and pulled himself to his feet, feeling the ache in his bones from the hours he'd sat at its base. He was bound by a rawhide thong that passed around the pole and to each wrist. By keeping his arms outstretched he could move about the pole like an animal on a leash. An army scout, Tap was called 'Many Speaks' by the Indians because he spoke the language of several tribes and he replied to Buffalo Lance in Sioux. "I didn't lie to you, Buffalo Lance..."

"Liar! Two-tongues!" the Indian screamed, cutting Tap's words short. Buffalo Lance carried a coup stick, a flat piece of wood about two feet long. It was colored red with vegetable dye and studded with brass tack heads. The warrior brought it down hard across Tap's face and shoulder.

The skin on his cheek stinging, Tap ducked away from a second blow. Buffalo Lance followed him around to the other side of the pole. The firelight played on the war paint that

1

proclaimed his readiness to die...or to deal out death.

Buffalo Lance was half a head shorter than the white man and his broad chest and flat face contrasted with Tap's leanness of flesh. Both men shared one feature--a strong, prominent nose. The Indian continued to stalk Tap as the white man circled about the pole, trying to keep out of reach of the coup stick. It wasn't a lethal weapon but it carried a bite and had raised a welt across Tap's cheek.

Tap circled half way around the post, putting his back to the two or three nearby tipis sitting on the edge of the camp, the darkness of the trees only a short distance beyond the light of the fire. The flames danced shadows of the two men across the buffalo hide cones as one pursued the other.

Meanwhile, gathered around, the tribe's warriors watched and waited, their faces golden-red circles in the firelight. It would be entertaining to see what fate was to befall the white man. Behind them, and spilling out on either end of the line of warriors, the camp's women and children also took in the spectacle.

Slowly, carefully, as if each step was measured out, Buffalo Lance circled the lodgepole. Tap mimicked his movements on the far side, ignoring the pain in his wrists as the rawhide thongs chafed and grated his skin. The fear of death--and a highly unpleasant one--overwhelmed any concern he might have for what pain the rawhide could inflict. He tried to think of a way to deflect Buffalo Shield's anger but before he could speak the brave suddenly stepped forward. With a cat-like movement he again struck out with the coup stick, slashing down across Tap's back.

"You told the soldiers where our camp would be!" he yelled, his voice nearly cracking with rage. "You led them to us! It's because of you our women weep and our young men die!"

Tap ducked low and scurried to the other side of the post, his eyes fastened on Buffalo Lance. Dammit! he said to himself, smelling the fear boiling out of his buckskin shirt and mingling with the dust both men were kicking up. Tap wasn't given to being made afraid easily but he'd seen the bodies of men who had been treated to Indian torture. A quick death he could bear but if Buffalo Lance wanted to extend his suffering...well, the Sioux had some interesting ways of doing so.

Buffalo Lance tracked along behind Tap, his steps unhastened, each made with great deliberation, the coup stick held ready. "Buffalo Lance! Once you called me brother! I've come to your camp as a friend..."

"You aren't a brother!" the Indian shot back at him. "You betrayed us to the soldiers. You told them we'd be on Old Man Creek. You caused the death of my son."

"No, Buffalo Lance!" Tap shouted. "I scout for the army but I wouldn't lead soldiers to a camp I knew was peaceful..."

"Liar!" the Indian yelled again, flailing away with the coup stick while Tap tried to scramble out of the way. The Indians had piled brush near the pole and as Tap moved he kicked at it, trying to push it away. He knew full well what it was for.

Tap kept to his awkward dance, changing positions, trying to stay away from Buffalo Lance. Beyond the campfire the night air was cool but here, near the fire--and under Buffalo Lance's fury--Tap was sweating, hard. He knew the Indians saw it and he tried to keep his features as stolid as he could under their studied--and passive--gaze. If he had to die he'd prefer to die as a man and not show the white feather...but it wasn't going to be easy.

In one of his circuits about the pole Tap recognized two men who had moved out of the shadows and were now standing apart from the others. One was Wolf Whistle, the band's chief. Next to him was Horse Catcher, a war chief like Buffalo Lance and head of the Arrow Bundle Society. They held their blankets tight about, their eyes impassive, their faces without expression. Both men had smoked the pipe with Tap in times past but now, under the sway of Buffalo Lance's anger, they were silent. Along with the others, they watched to see what punishment this white man would receive at the hands of Buffalo Lance, leader of the Red Fox Society.

Buffalo Lance backed away from the lodgepole, his face still an immobile mask of rage. He walked over to the fire and reached down to it, seemingly taking great care in picking out a burning brand from the flames.

3

"Only you, Many Speaks, knew we were camped on Old Man Creek. Only you could have told Two Bars where to find us." The Indian held up a burning brand. "You said you were my brother. Now you will die for your lies!"

Sweat soaked Tap's shirt and it wasn't all from the fire. Fighting back the panic he worked at the leather thong that secured his wrists to the lodgepole, turning the skin raw and red. "Goddammit, Buffalo Lance!" Tap shouted in English, knowing the warrior understood his words. "I'm a friend of the Cheyenne, the Sioux, the Comanche." He rummaged his mind for words that would let him break through the Indians wrath. "I've fought with you against the Crow! Even against the soldiers, once! I wouldn't betray you!"

There was a sinking feeling in the pit of Tap's stomach as Buffalo Lance approached him with the brand. His face was hard and cold and his eyes shone like the dark, polished agates of the necklace he wore about his neck. He wasn't listening to Tap's words. "My son die," he said, speaking also in English. "My brother bleeds in his lodge from soldier guns. His wives cry for him."

Buffalo Lance stood only feet away, the flaming branch in one hand, his coup stick in the other. As stoic as his face was, it held all the grief and fury that thirty-odd years of watching the white invaders move onto his land could instill. He was not in a mood to hear what he considered more white men's lies. Still in English, he said, "This what I think of your words!"

Buffalo Lance lofted the burning branch into the brush behind Tap's feet. With a muffled report the dry branches blossomed into flames, leaping into the dark sky. Tap kicked out at the burning tangle of sage with one foot, the fire licking around the old fashioned over-the-knee cavalry boots he wore. Shying from the fire, he ducked his face under one arm and raised his hands above his head. Tap tried to jump high enough to bring the leather thong over the top of the lodgepole but it was several feet too high. He kicked at another clump of brush that ignited with a blush of red and yellow, searing him through the thick blue wool soldier's trousers and the leather shirt he wore. Behind him several braves laughed. One stepped forward and

4

used a coup stick to push some of the burning brush back toward the lodgepole and the white man dancing about it, trying to escape.

Buffalo Lance stood nearby. He was no further from the fire than Tap but he ignored the heat, as if to purge his own anguish in the flames that would soon consume the scout. Tap, his hands still held high, put all his weight against the leather thongs on his wrists, trying to break the rawhide bonds. Fear and desperation surged through him. It was unlike anything he'd ever felt before, even in the height of battle during the War.

Smoke was starting to curl off the fabric of Tap's trousers as more flaming brush was pushed toward the pole. There was no way he was going to die in quiet dignity like an Indian warrior would. He was quickly descending into a blind panic that blotted out everything else...almost.

Tap heard the high, keening wail, like that made by some night bird. If any of the Sioux heard it, they must have dismissed the sound. But not Tap. It was Whittiker!

Tap tried to ignore the flames, struggling to concentrate on the man out in the dark. His eyes frantic, he searched the black between the lodges at Buffalo Lance's back. Then, in the firelight, Tap saw a flash as a tomahawk shot out of the night beyond the tipis and slammed into the lodgepole, severing the rawhide cord.

Tap still had his weight on the leather thong and he almost fell backward into the fire. He caught himself and reached up, grabbing the tomahawk. Behind him, their view obscured by the smoke, most of the braves were unaware of his being cut loose. However Buffalo Lance, standing close by, saw. A look of surprise crossed his face but he quickly shook it off and ran forward, the coup stick held high.

Tap rushed toward him, taking the blow across his shoulder. In return he swung the tomahawk, catching Buffalo Lance along side the head with the flat and sending him sprawling. Two long bounds later he was free of the circle of fire and he headed for the tipis on the edge of the camp still a few yards away, a feeling of elation washing over him that almost made his knees buckle. Wolf Whistle and Horse Catcher, belatedly realizing what was

5

happening, started after him.

"To yer right! Yer right!" someone shouted out of the dark and Tap grinned at the old man's voice. Whittiker, he thought, when this is over I'm going to give you a big kiss, your whiskers unwashed or not.

Tap ran for the lodges to his right. He disappeared into the darkness between them just as a series of shots rattled out of the black on the other side of the tipi. They were squirted out, Tap knew, by Whittiker working the lever of his yellow-boy '66 Winchester as fast as he could. The shots were aimed high, more to confuse than to cause injury. It was an attempt to slow down the rest of the Sioux who were coming around the backside of the fire to see what was happening.

"Many Speaks is getting away!" one yelled, and the cry was taken up by others. Shots were now coming from the camp, seeking out Tap...and Whittiker, still somewhere in the darkness.

Tap heard Whittiker shout again. "Keep goin'! Follow the moon!" and Tap continued his stumbled run. He wasn't able to see in the dark but he took a sighting on the half-moon that rose over the hills ahead. Suddenly he crashed into the side of something.

The 'something' reared and snorted, prancing about and Tap grabbed at the leather strap that held the horse to a nearby tree. His eyes were beginning to adjust to the moonlight and he saw a second animal nearby. Then, without a sound, a figure slithered out of the brush. Whittiker!

"Hey, old son," the man cackled, "Hope I didn't spoil yer fun. Looks like they was holding a bar-bee-que, all just fer you."

"Shut up, you old goat!" Tap growled, affectionately. "I was almost fried before you tossed that hatchet!" He swung up into the McClellen saddle, Whittiker matching him as he brought his long frame into the old Spanish kak he preferred to ride, the Winchester in his right hand.

Both men glanced back to the camp, the tipis nearest them outlined by the campfire and the now-blazing death fire beyond. Sioux were boiling out around the lodges and more shouts--and shots--flitted through the air. Both men knew that in a moment they could expect to be pursued as those warriors that had the forethought to stake their favorite war ponies outside their lodges gave chase.

"Ain't no time fer long good-byes," the old scout said, shoving a few shells into the Winchester's loading gate. "Head off to yer right, bearin' on the moon, and we'll be out on the flats. Then, fifteen interestin' miles to the fort."

Tap heard a 'whoosh' as they both turned their horses and gave spur. There was another such sound and then a third...and Tap reeled forward in the saddle. "I'm hit!" he cried.

But Whittiker was too far ahead to hear and there wasn't any chance to stop now and see how badly off he was anyway...unless he wanted to add his scalp to Buffalo Lance's belt. The horse didn't need any urging or guidance. It was more than willing to follow the other cavalry mount and get away from the strange sounds and smells of the Indian camp.

Tap felt up and around to his left shoulder and to the arrow shaft he found there. He'd been hit high up, into the shoulder blade. He could only guess that the Indian who'd fired the arrow was either too far away or hadn't had time to take a good pull on the bow. A strap-iron arrow point was capable of going clear through his shoulder and out the other side. Just the same, it was starting to hurt like hell and the pain made him double up, his face against the horse's straining neck. With the animal pounding along under him, each jar sent a stab of pain through his body.

In a few minutes they were out on the open prairie and he pushed himself up from the saddle. Ahead he could see Whittiker, pulling back from their mad dash and now maintaining a ground-eating canter. They had an almost two-hour ride to Fort McPherson. Still, the Indian ponies shouldn't be able to catch up with them. The Sioux horses were just coming off a long winter and had yet to fatten up to their full strength. The hay and grain fed animals both scouts were mounted on, while not as tough as the Sioux horses, would prevail in this kind of test.

The two men came abreast and Whittiker looked over and grinned, the moonlight making his craggy face appear like some sort of bearded gargoyle as he raised his rifle high. Tap nodded

7

at the man and then slumped back over the cantle. Whittiker moved ahead, still unaware of his companion's plight. For most of the ride into McPherson Tap was hunched over the saddle, propping himself up with his right arm, his other arm, along with the left side of his body, almost useless from the pain of the arrow. Somewhere in the last half hour into the fort he must have passed out, maintaining his seat by second nature alone.

The next thing Tap knew he was in a bed in the post infirmary.

2

Fort McPherson was set on a flat, nearly treeless section of land in the eastern part of Dakota Territory. Close by ran a small tributary of the Knife River called Coyote Creek. The fort, named for a general killed during the battle of Atlanta, had been completed the year before, in 1874. It still smelled of new-cut wood...mixed with the pungent odor of manure since it was the home of the 17th U.S. Cavalry, companies C and D. It was a non-stockaded fort, laid out in a 'U' pattern around a central parade ground.

Once past the twin posts that flanked the entrance, on the left border of the parade ground, was a row of buildings that served as the quarters for the officers and men--Officer's Row. Directly ahead, at the far extremes of the grounds, sat the commanding officer's quarters, mess, administration and quartermaster stores. Lined out on the right side, forming the final leg of the 'U,' were the post trader and various other supply buildings. The last building in this leg, as if tagged on by afterthought, was the post surgeon's house. The infirmary made up the back of this building...

"What...?" Tap said, opening his eyes with a start to see Colonel Bruster standing at the foot of his bed.

"So. Returned from the Land of Nod," the fort commander said, smiling down at Tap from a round open face that sported a ferocious set of graying muttonchops.

Tap pushed himself up and then fell back with a groan, a stab of pain in his shoulder reminding him of the arrow. He ran a hand down through his dark brown hair and over a face long and lean and covered with several days of stubble.

"How long have I been here?"

The colonel reached into a pocket and fished out a watch. "Well, according to this old turnip, about ten hours. Whittiker brought you in a little after one in the morning and it's eleven-fifteen now."

"How am I?"

9

"You took an arrow in the shoulder. Up high." The colonel's tone was light, as if he was referring to a mosquito bite. "Surgeon Gates said the point turned when it hit your shoulder blade. Had to mess up a little meat getting it out, but you can return to duty tomorrow. Just watch for infection."

Tap shoved himself up again and swung his long legs over the edge of the bed, one of four in a little room that reeked of carbolic and also served for any operations Doctor Gates had to perform. He pulled off the shreds of his undergarment and reached out for the buckskin shirt on the neighboring bunk. It was splotched with blood and split up the back.

"Here, I brought this from your kit," the colonel said, handing Tap a collarless white flannel shirt and then sitting on the adjoining bunk.

Tap undid the buttons at the top and shrugged the shirt over his head...carefully. Then he stood and pulled on his trousers-- the colonel helped with the left side--and again sat down. He picked up his over-the-knee boots. "I'll play hell getting these on with one wing puny."

"Thought of that too." The colonel dropped a pair of current-pattern cavalry boots on the floor next to Tap. "Had Sergeant Quinn size your boots and pull a pair from stores. The government can get the cost back out of your next pay."

"Thanks," Tap said, shrugging into the new boots with his good arm.

"Why do you still wear those things?" asked Bruster. "Other than Bill Cody, I didn't think anyone wore them anymore."

"Well, they're still in good shape. Almost like new."

"New!" Bruster snorted. "When did you have them made?"

Tap thought a moment. "Just before the Wilderness Campaign. In Virginia. Right after I was ordered to scout for your brigade."

"That was in April of sixty-four!"

"I said they were good boots. Cost me an arm and a leg."

"Speaking of losing body parts," the colonel said, "what happened out there?" Bruster inclined his head toward the wall and, by extension, the open country beyond.

10

Tap stood, moving about the small room, trying out the boots...and his shoulder. "Well, Whittiker figured it'd been a heap of years since I scouted around this country so he was giving me the grand tour, over toward the Knife River. When we hit the Knife, we thought maybe we'd look about and see if we could cut some wagon tracks...maybe from those gun runners you want me to find...or Indian sign. So we split up, Whittiker going east and me going west, upstream."

Tap spotted his 'possibles' bag on the bunk with his shredded rawhide jacket. He was surprised to see it. The bag had been on his saddle and he'd supposed one of Buffalo Lance's men would have taken it. He opened the bag and took out a curved pipe and some tobacco and proceeded to build a bowlful of smoke.

"After about a half-hour ride I ran across a Sioux warrior I know...Buffalo Lance. Him and some of his warriors were out doing a little spring hunting. Buffalo Lance is kind of a hardcase...always wanting to start trouble, even when it's not called for."

Tap sat down again on the cot. He was still a little dizzy from his exertions. "Didn't worry me, though. I was in his camp, visiting Horse Catcher, another war chief, a few weeks before I left Rice. Peaceful enough then. So, when they pulled me off my horse, trussed me up and took me to their camp, I was a mite surprised."

"Where was his camp? Near here?" Bruster asked.

"About fifteen miles north," Tap said. "They've probably moved by now. That's where Buffalo Lance--he's a war chief and leader of the Red Fox Society--blamed me for causing that raid I hear Captain Hawthorne made last week, when I was on my way here from Rice." There was more than a hint of accusation in Tap's voice at the mention of the posts' Chief of Scouts but Bruster ignored it.

"Did you see any repeaters in his camp?"

"Yeah," Tap said. "Most hadn't even been decorated up with brass tacks or some-such yet, like they usually get around to doing. Was mostly Spencers and sixty-six Winchesters...and" Tap made a face, "mine joined them." Tap tilted his head,

11

looking across the bunk at the colonel. "Don't suppose you have any spare repeaters here...?"

"No. Quartermasters had to turn in all our Spencers for Springfields last year." Bruster stood up again. "Well, I want you to make it your job to find out where these rifles are coming from. Not perform routine scouting,"

"That kind of work, maybe you want the Pinkertons," Tap said.

"I want Pinkerton's who can scout...or scouts who can think like Pinkerton's. And with your lawman background..."

"That was just town marshall work in a couple hell-on-wheels trail camps. Not real detective work!"

"Just the same," Bruster said, his voice firm, "That's why I sent for you. Look for guns, not Sioux. Find out where they come from." The colonel stood, his expression showing the matter was settled. "I have Whittiker and Forsyth if I need a scout at a column's head."

"And by-the-by. When you're done here, report to Captain Hawthorne. After all, he is Chief of Scouts and deserves the courtesy of a report from you."

Then the colonel's voice changed tone, becoming almost light hearted as a smile brightened his face. "But now for some pleasant news. My daughter, Matty, arrived yesterday. I knew she was coming of course, but I wanted to surprise you. I remember how well you and Matty got along back when she was just a girl, visiting me before the Wilderness Campaign. I'll go get her. She's been waiting outside until you were decent."

Bruster stopped at the door and looked back at Tap. "I think Captain Hawthorne had something to do with her coming here. Before he was assigned to McPherson, he was stationed at Jefferson Barracks, Missouri, where Matty's been staying with her aunt." He winked and went through the door while a thousand near-forgotten thoughts boiled up out of Tap's memory.

3

It was in late April of 1864 when Tap had first met Matty. He had been assigned to scout for a brigade led by Bruster--then a one-star general of volunteers. The brigade was part of the Army of the Potomac, itself nominally under the command of General Meade, but in actuality, driven by Grant. Grant was starting to prepare for the move across Virginia's Rapidan River. He would soon engage Lee's Army of Northern Virginia, encamped somewhere south of the Rapidan. It would lead to a macabre dance of death as the two armies first wheeled about each other in a tangle of second-growth timber known as the Wilderness and then fought on to Spotsylvania and the Bloody Angle.

In the few weeks before the army moved south Tap met Bruster's daughter, Matty, a headstrong and determined young woman who insisted in following her father to the fringes of battle.

Matty was only seventeen but she was very much a woman, tall and full figured with a mass of auburn hair above luminous hazel eyes. Tap had been barely nineteen years old himself at the time and the two had hit it right off despite Tap's shyness around women. Tap and Matty had spent many hours together in the weeks before Grant moved the army south--and in moments stolen away from army duty in the eleven months to follow that led up to the fall of Petersburg.

The door to the little infirmary opened and Tap looked up, his throat strangely dry. Then Matty was across the room and into his arms. She gave him a kiss that told him that perhaps not as much time had fled past as he had thought...at least as far as their passions were concerned.

"M-Matty!" he said holding her away from him, using his left arm despite the stab of pain that went down his back. "I, I..."

"Well! Is that all you can say after eleven years?" she said, her eyes almost closing as a smile lit up her face. She was fashionably outfitted in a dark gray bustled dress and a paletot top. On her head, tilted to one side, sat a small hat in matching gray. Except that her hair was a shade darker, to Tap she looked the same as when he'd last seen her, shortly after the war's end.

Matty put a hand on his arm, turning him around. Her voice now serious, "I was told you'd been wounded in some terrible battle with the Indians. "You are all right, aren't you?"

"Ye-yes! Just a light wound...what are you doing out here?"

"Oh, you know me! I always want to be with the Colonel. I followed him through most of the war and I'm still following him." She brightened up her face--and the room--with another smile. "Maybe that's why I've never let a man pin me down to marriage. I'm married to the army."

She moved closer to Tap. "But I remember one man who could have stolen my heart...a dashing young cavalier who rode like a centaur and swept away this Yankee belle..."

"Matty! That was years ago...you were just...a girl...we were just...friends," Tap lied to himself. He damn well knew that they had been more than 'friends.'

She twirled away from him. "Did I seem like 'just a girl' when we were together...alone?" Matty said, giving him a coquettish smile.

Tap blushed and tripped over his tongue again. "Now don't...I don't...I mean..,"

Matty stepped to the door. "Well, we'll see, my dashing, gallant scout," she said, her voice almost sounding a musical note. "I'll be here at Fort McPherson as long as the Colonel is in command. And remember, there's a post ball in a few days. I'll expect you to escort me to the dance floor more than once."

Tap remembered something the colonel said. "What about Captain Hawthorne?" His voice held a trace of something-- jealousy?--and it surprised him to hear it. "I've heard he has some place in your affections."

Matty wrinkled her small, upturned nose and walked back to take Tap by the hand.

"What Captain Hawthorne assumes and what is actual may be two different things," she replied. "I'll be seeing you again, Tap Duncan. Soon!"

She lifted herself up on tip-toe again and gave him a quick kiss on the lips. Then she was gone through the door. He heard her light footsteps cross the floor and fade away out the front door. He leaned back against the wall. Matty! After all these years!

At the war's end he had thought of asking for her hand in marriage. But then he realized the futility of such a hope. Matty was a general's daughter and he owned nothing other than the horse that he rode. So he had returned to the frontier where he had grown up. Maybe there he could make his fortune in gold mining or the taking of hides...perhaps even at the gaming tables.

How often, in those first years after the war, had he yearned for her, to be with her, to touch her. But time had slipped by--as had the chances for fortune--and the adventure of the new land had taken hold of him and the dream of Matty had faded from his mind...until now. He was surprised--and a little shaken--to discover how strong his feelings for her still were.

He moved himself out of the infirmary and into the dimly lit doctor's office, through the door and onto the porch. Tap pulled his hat down against the glare of the sun and remembered the colonel's suggestion he report to Hawthorne.

4

The captain's office was a hundred yards away in one of the buildings fronting the parade grounds and given over to the fort's Headquarters and Staff. It was next to, but separate from, the building where Bruster had his office. Tap mounted to the porch that ran the length of the building's front, opened the door and stepped into a hallway that led past several small rooms used by various officers. The smell of green wood, cigar smoke and strong coffee--brewed in a pot on a nearby stove--mingled in the stale air. The first door on Tap's left was Captain Hawthorne's and he knocked--then opened the door at a gruff reply.

Hawthorne sat at a small desk with his back to the side wall of the building. He looked up as Tap closed the door behind him.

"Scout Duncan reporting as directed by the colonel..." Tap began but Hawthorne cut him short with a gesture, standing as he broke in.

"What the hell were you doing out there scouting down Indians?" Hawthorne said, accusingly. "Your orders were to look for gun runners."

Hawthorne leaned over his desk, propping himself on his arms. He was in his mid-thirties, a tall man with sharp, angular features, not the least bit softened by the sallow mustache drooping down around the corner's of his mouth like a pair of yellow pinchers. His uniform, carefully tailored beyond what a captain's pay would normally allow, fitted his slender frame like a glove.

"I didn't find any Indians," Tap retorted, "they found me. And thanks to that raid you made on a hide drying party a few weeks back, I damn near ended up fried meat!"

"Raid? I...that was an attack on a hostile village!" Hawthorne stammered. "You know very well the War Department has declared all Indians who are outside their designated reservations without agent approval to be hostile and open to attack. That band," he added, stiffly, "did not have permission to be off their reservation."

"Chrissakes, Hawthorne!" Tap said, his voice rising, ignoring the fact that, as Chief of Scouts, the captain was his superior. "Those were just women and kids and a couple older boys who weren't even warriors yet. And you killed four of them--including Buffalo Lances' son." Tap crossed the short distance to the desk and stood in front of Hawthorne, almost eye-to-eye.

"If Whittiker hadn't come along when he did," Tap said, his voice still at an elevated pitch, "I'd be ashes blowing across the prairie right now. You want a step up in rank? Don't do it by killing peacefulls!"

Stung, Hawthorne came around the desk, his own face starting to redden, his voice ratchetting up to match Tap's. "That had nothing to do with my actions," He started. "I was just doing my duty..."

"Well killing women and children is damn poor duty," Tap threw back at him, matching anger for anger. "Now Buffalo Lance is pushing for Wolf Whistle's band to go to war. Wolf Whistle is peaceful and so's Horse Catcher...but I dunno. Horse Catcher had a sister hurt in that raid. Buffalo Lance wants the different bands to get together. It happens," Tap swung his arm in an arc--and grimaced as he was immediately reminded of the hole in his shoulder, "we have an Indian war on our hands."

"I think you had better leave Indian policy to the Army," Hawthorne said, testily. "And," he added, "I think you had better leave Miss Bruster to officer's row."

Tap was taken back and he stammered, "Wha...what! What the hell do you mean by that...?"

"I saw Miss Bruster come out of the surgeon's quarters...after her father left." Hawthorne stepped to the window and looked out over the parade ground, his back to Tap. "I understand you knew her during the war--when she was only a girl." Hawthorne turned around to face Tap again. "But she is a colonel's daughter. Hardly the kind of young lady to be associated with a some common squaw-man."

Tap spoke slowly. "Seems you assume an awful lot of late. Like peaceful Indians held to slaughter, just to get you nudged up the promotion list. Or." Tap's eyes narrowed, "a woman

18

being yours because of the bars you wear."

The captain was still for a moment, then turned away from the window and moved near the desk, facing the scout. Tap could see his words had stung Hawthorne who was struggling to keep control of his emotions. Slowly Hawthorne pulled free a set of gauntlets hanging on his belt. Tap looked down at them and then at Hawthorne's face, working to contain his anger.

"You mean to call up a duel with them gloves, you might think twice," Tap warned. "Those things touch my face, I'll put you out into the parade ground, right through that window."

The blow of the gloves across his face surprised Tap but at the same time galvanized him into action. He threw a right that caught the captain along the side of his face, driving him back against the desk. Tap tried to follow it up with a left but the pain from his wound stifled the motion and Hawthorne brought the heavy leather gauntlets down across his face again. It was a stinging blow that tore water from Tap's eyes.

Temporarily blinded, Tap threw his arms around Hawthorne, tying him up as they collided with the desk and turned it over. They staggered about, Hawthorne delivering a series of short punches to Tap's midsection, the only real damage he could do while his arms were pinned. Tap, for his part, tried to ram Hawthorne's spine into the edge of the overturned desk. The pain in his shoulder made him unable to do much else beyond restraining Hawthorne's arms.

The two continued to thrash across the room, scattering chairs and knocking a bookcase over. The stomp and heave of their boots on the wooden floor accentuated the grunts and intakes of air their exertions forced from them. Then there was a distant bang as the front door flew open and next the office door swung back and someone was pulling them apart.

"Gents! Gents! Ya both want a courts martial?"

Tap moved away from Hawthorne, wiping his eyes. He looked at Quinn, the post's first sergeant. The non-com, a short, burly man with the stripes of twenty years in the army on his shirt sleeve, stood between them, one hand outstretched to each, acting as a barrier. Hawthorne shot a hate-filled look at Tap and then turned and strode out the door, his gauntlets still grasped

19

tight in his hand.

Quinn looked at Tap. "You OK?" At Tap's nod Quinn righted the desk and quickly began to pick up the scattered books.

Tap waited a few seconds, to give Hawthrone a chance to clear the building. Then he stepped out of the office, went down the hallway and out onto the porch, his breathing still heavy. Hawthorne was nowhere in sight. He leaned against a porch overhang support for a moment, then slid down to rest on the steps. His legs felt wobbly and his shoulders seemed to carry a weariness that wasn't just from his wound. Buffalo Lance was out to kill him, there were gunrunners to track down and an Indian war was in the making. Now Matty had suddenly reappeared in his life along with a jealous suitor who also happened to be an army officer. He should have stayed at Fort Rice, he thought. Life was simpler there.

Tap finally roused himself from the porch steps. He was now being assailed by a pain in his gut that rivaled the one in his back--it hit him that it had been almost twenty-four hours since he'd eaten. Tap walked down to the Post Trader--though he referred to it by the term used during the War--the sutlers--and bought a can of peaches and a beef sandwich that the trader made for him. Tap was dying for a beer but Bruster had set strict times for liquor sales and it would be a few hours before the store could sell him any.

By the time he'd crossed the parade grounds and mounted the steps to the scout's quarters Tap had wolfed down the sandwich. The little building sat near the camp's entrance, at the end of Officer's Row. Made of rough-sawn boards, it was just big enough for the three bunks and a small wood stove that were crammed into it. The only other amenity it held was a row of shelves, up high, along the back wall, to hold the scout's belongings. Tap kicked the door shut as a voice sounded out.

"Hey, old son! Up and about, are ya?"

Tap crossed the room and, one hand still clutching the peaches, swung his arms around the shoulders of the tall, craggy-faced old man who stood there. "Whittiker, you old son-of-a-bitch! If it wasn't for you, my bones would be getting gnawed on by Indian dogs right about now."

"All in a day's work. Shoot! I didn't even realize you'd taken an arrer until we was only a half-hour out from the fort. Stopped and lashed you down so you wouldn't fall off." The old man cackled. "Brought you in over yer saddle like a dressed-out elk!"

"Speaking of horses," Tap said, starting to work on the peachtin lid with his jackknife, "how did you get mine back?"

Whittiker sat back down on his bunk, returning to the rifle he'd been cleaning. "Was almost dark when I backtracked you to the Injun camp. I scouted about and saw your horse tied back of a lodge. Had Buffalo Lances' shield outside so musta been his place. All the Injuns was at the other end of camp, waitin' fer you to amuse them so's I grabbed the horse." Whittiker ran a hand over his short white beard. "Figured, if I have to tie a couple animals off a ways, wanted them friendly-like. I try to tie a strange Injun pony with mine, they'd be buck-snortin' around somethin' fierce."

Tap pointed to several firearms--Whittiker's personal arsenal, a scattergun and two rifles--leaning against the wall by the old scout's bunk. "Don't suppose you could spare one of those rifles until I can get a new one?"

"Hell yes! Take the Spencer. Got ten tubes fer 'er too." He handed Tap a leather pouch full of ammunition tubes. "All loaded."

"Thanks," Tap said. "Here, help yourself." He handed the now-open tin of peaches to Whittiker. The old scout reached behind him and pulled out a huge Bowie knife with a blade at least a foot long. He rammed the blade down into the can, bringing it out with half the peach halves impaled on it.

"Thankee, old son," he said, returning the tin. "Don't mind if'n I do!" He ate a peach half off the blade of the knife, turning it as he chewed around the peach. Then he wiped a sleeve across his mouth.

"Unnerstand you and Hawthorne had a set-to..."

"Huh! That was about a half hour ago. "How'd you learn of it?"

"Small post. Not much news. Any we git, got quick legs." Whittiker started working on another peach. "Bad blood between you two? Musta been from before. You ain't been at 'Pherson long enough to work up that size a mad..."

Tap nodded his head, putting the Spencer against the wall by his bunk and settling back on the blankets. "Goes back a ways. I was scouting for the Seventh in sixty-eight, trying to track down a Cheyenne raiding party that hit Kansas and made off with some white captives. The trail led to Black Kettle's band, on the Washita. I told Custer that Black Kettle was peaceful...it was him and his people who were almost all killed off for no reason at Sand Creek when they got jumped by Colorado Militia."

Tap took out his pipe. His voice was taking on an edge and

22

a smoke would help calm him. "I about had him convinced that the raiding party mightn't be from Black Kettle's bunch. They could be just passing through. Figured we owed Black Kettle that much benefit of the doubt."

"I was willing to go in alone and talk it out with Black Kettle first. I wasn't too worried. I spent a summer living in his camp when I was just a kid. They were friends of mine."

Tap inhaled and held the smoke for several seconds before expelling it into the air. "Hawthorne, who was a lieutenant than, leading a troop, argued him out of it. Said we'd lose the element of surprise. Ended up, we killed some forty women and children and got the captives killed to boot."

Tap took in and blew out another angry cloud of smoke. "But, by damn! The next promotion list that came down, Hawthorne had his captaincy!"

6

Tap spent the rest of the day in the scout's quarters, resting his shoulder and keeping away from both Hawthorne and Matty. The next day he decided to ride into Demerest, the nearest town. In part, he wanted to remove himself from the fort for awhile so he wouldn't have to deal with either Hawthorne or Matty directly...and when he stepped out the door those were the first two people he saw.

It was a mild spring morning and the sun wasn't more than an hour over the horizon. Matty and the captain moved at a light trot from the direction of officer's row. The colonel's daughter was mounted sidesaddle on a little bay while Captain Hawthorne escorted her on a large roan. Matty was dressed in a blue riding habit and she sat the saddle with ease, a riding crop in one hand.

"Good morning, Scout Duncan," Matty said sweetly as she rode by.

Tap, dumbfounded, could only dredge up a garbled "'Mornin' Miss Bruster," and damn near choked on that. Hawthorne, for his part, stared straight ahead, as if Tap wasn't there. Clear of the gate, where a trooper saluted them, they moved off at an easy lope. Tap didn't miss the picnic basket that the captain had slung over one arm.

Carrying the Spencer and some loose cartridges--he didn't like fooling with the fragile tubes--Tap headed for the stable, grumbling to himself. What the hell was Matty doing going off with Hawthorne after what she had said to him the day before? And with hostile Indians around? He hoped Hawthorne kept close to the fort.

Tap rounded the surgeon's quarters and headed for a long horse shed fifty feet to the rear. A sheltering overhang protected the front of the shed and a series of hitching posts ran its length. It was here the troopers saddled up when called to mounted duty. The shed itself held stalls for a few personal mounts belonging to the officers. Off to one side, near a holding pen, Tap saw Sergeant Quinn talking to a man who, though dressed in white men's clothes, looked to be an Indian. Quinn broke off the conversation and walked over to meet Tap as the other man walked away.

"One of the 'Ree scouts? Tap Asked, referring to the Arikara scouts assigned to McPherson.

"No," the sergeant said, running his hand through a thinning crop of hair. "Just a blanket Indian who hangs around. Does odd jobs. Told him I didn't have anything for him today." Like most frontier army posts it was the first sergeant who saw to the running of the camp and little was done that didn't have his stamp of approval first.

Quinn pointed to a stall in the long shed. "Joshua is in number eight. Figured, after the long haul in the other night, didn't need him to be out milling around with the rest of the nags."

"Thanks," Tap said, heading for the stall. "If he looks rested up, I'll use him instead of Jericho" He nodded toward a pen holding--along with government horses--the other animal that he brought from Fort Rice.

"You don't use Jericho much. Ought to sell him to the colonel. He's broke to drive and he'd look smart hitched to the Colonel's buggy."

"I use him when I got distance to cover," Tap said. "Got lots of bottom. Only problem, he's a bit headstrong. Sometimes, get in a tight, he don't always want to do what you want him too."

A soldier on stable duty, anticipating Tap, met him halfway with the horse. Tap proceeded to lead the big dun around. The horse pranced and snorted and Tap could see he was happy to be out of the confines of the stall. "Looks fine." He turned to the soldier. "Mind grabbing my saddle?"

Ten minutes later Tap was at a lope, moving through the post gate and heading for Demerest. He scanned the ground, making sure he wasn't on a track to overtake Matty and the captain. Their trail soon turned off toward the north while Demerest was south-west of the fort. Probably heading for a nice treed spot along the creek to picnic, he thought and the idea sent a wave of anger through him. He kicked the horse into a brief gallop...but soon pulled back, mindful of the numerous prairie dog holes that dotted the ground.

The day had looked to be warm and Tap had responded by wearing only a light cotton shirt, a blue bandana to hide its lack of collar, his blue wool cavalry trousers and a wide-brimmed hat. In an open-topped holster on his right hip he carried a new pattern Colt .45 with the cavalry-length barrel. It had replaced his trusty .36 Colt Navy just the year before. He carried extra rounds in an infantry cartridge pouch attached to a plain leather service belt. Out of concern for his shoulder he had lashed the Spencer to the back of the saddle rather than use the sling and carbine socket and allow it to bounce along his backside like a trooper would.

Tap's dark thoughts of Matty and the captain were suddenly interrupted by the sound of gunfire off to his left. They were loud, booming shots that rolled out over the prairie. Curious, he turned the horse in their direction.

The land along here rose and fell in gentle waves, no sooner did a rider top one earthen crest than he was into the trough of the next swale. Tap came out of one trough, hit the crest--and pulled up, sharply. Below him unfolded a sight that he'd seen more than once but that always took his breath away. The land before him stopped rolling. It spread out into a gentle falling plain as far as he could see. Scattered about it, also to the horizon, was an immense herd of buffalo, their wooly bodies blanketing the prairie like some huge, living carpet. A couple of hundred yards ahead of him was a circle of freight wagons and a group of men lined out on the ground. Several manned heavy buffalo rifles, the muzzles supported by two crossed sticks driven into the ground--buffalo hiders.

The main portion of the herd ignored the shooting, moving at random over the grassy plain, grazing. Only a small band of animals a few hundred yards in front of the shooters--small in relation to the rest of the herd--was involved in the killing. Even these showed only some dim concern when one of their numbers collapsed under the onslaught of a five-hundred grain slug of lead. One or two might nose at the fallen body, but they didn't seem to comprehend the danger. As their companions continued to drop, there was no attempt to either move away or attack the hunters. Tap clicked his horse ahead and moved down toward the hiders.

He was spotted within seconds and all the men immediately turned toward him, bringing their guns around. When he moved closer and it became apparent he was a white man their concern abated and they relaxed. Obviously they were aware of the Indian unrest. Tap pulled up about fifty feet out. Even from here he was hit by the unmistakable stench of rotting flesh and green hides that always hung about a hider camp.

"'Morning," he said. "Getting many hides?"

A man who looked to be in his late thirties stepped forward. He was light complexioned, almost pink, and his features bordered on delicate. Against the cool of the morning he wore a gray military style coat. Tap could see the remaining strands of braid that once adorned a Confederate officer's uniform.

"'Mornin,'" the man replied with a soft Southern drawl. "Gettin' some." Care to step down and have a touch of coffee?" He tilted his head toward a nearby fire and a large enameled pot.

"Thanks, no. Heading for Demerest and the next thing I want down my throat is a beer."

The man in the coat stepped near, his hand extended up to Tap. "George Bell Hancock, late of the Sovereign State of Virginia, at your service, suh."

Tap took the hand, strong and firm despite the wan look of the man. "Tap Duncan. Scouting for the Seventeenth, out of Fort McPherson." Tap noticed the men with the rifles watching him. They were holding up their shooting to allow the two men to talk. "Didn't mean to stop your hunting," he said.

Hancock waved a hand. "That's all right. We've got more than our skinners can handle before they spoil now. Guess we shouldn't have killed so many but its been awhile since we've seen a herd this big. Wanted to get some practice in." The man shook his head. "Way it's going, buffalo are going to be quite scarce in another season or two."

"Don't suppose," Tap said, trying hard to keep the edge out of his voice, "you considered holding off a year. Let the buffalo breed back a bit?"

The man shook his head. "No. Someone else would just go out and kill them."

28

A hunter, sitting a few yards away with a Sharps across his lap, piped up. "It's like little Phil sez," he crowed. "Kill off the bufflers, ya solve the Injun problem." He laughed and then spit a wad of tobacco in the dust.

"Any chance you've seen wagon tracks out on the open grass," Tap said, changing the subject. "Or maybe track of pack animals?"

Hancock shook his head. "'Fraid not. We came out of Demerest on the military road and turned due east, to this herd, soon's we learned it moved into the country. That was two days ago." The man arched his eyebrows slightly. "Why? What're you looking for?"

"People running guns in. To the Indians."

The man looked reflective. "Well, I'd have a stake in stopping that sort of thing. If I see any tracks, I'll send a man over to the fort and have you notified."

"Much obliged," Tap said, reining his horse around. "Oh, by the way. There are some bands of Sioux out. Most are just looking to hunt, like you are. But a few could be hostile. Keep an eye open." The man waved as Tap set his horse in motion and the men with the rifles took up their grim harvest again.

The wanton killing distressed Tap. He had spent one season at it, in sixty-eight. It had looked like a good way to make some decent money fast. At the time he was still thinking of Matty and his desire to return to her with a stake in his poke. Half a season of slaughter had been all he could take. His having lived with the Sioux and the Cheyenne while growing up, on the then-frontier's edge of Minnesota and Iowa, had taught him just what the great, shaggy beasts meant to the Plains Tribes.

The Souix and the Cheyenne revered the buffalo more than any other object--more even than their ponies. The Indian world was centered around the mystical, migrating animal that furnished them with almost every necessity; food, tools, clothing, and most important, their religion. The little hunter with the Sharps had been right in quoting General Phil Sheriden--when the buffalo were gone, the Indian would be gone too, at least as a separate nation. Then, in the words of another General--Sherman--they would become either a specie of pauper, dependent on the government...or all be killed off.

The thought of the plains devoid of buffalo with all the tribes sitting in reservations filled him with sorrow. It would leave the once-proud warriors to decay away into impoverished blanket clutchers for the Eastern tourists to gawk at. He felt all the more bad about it because, in scouting for the army, he was helping to further that end.

Demerest was about fifteen miles from the fort and the spring rains had turned parts of the road into a rutted cowpath-- passable but Joshua had better footing in the grass. Avoiding the road, Tap continued to ride across the open prairie. About five miles from the town he pulled up at a set of tracks weaving through the long grass. They were deep but not the tracks of a heavy freight wagon--more like an army ambulance, loaded down. He figured they were at least four days old...maybe a week. From the sign there were two vehicles, both pulled by large teams of mules heading, more or less, toward the town. Tap thought on that. It would take mules--or horses--to move heavy wagon loads fast over that kind of ground. Still, why would anyone hauling normal freight risk bogging down, or getting hit by Indians, when the road, as rutted as it was, would be easier and was patrolled to boot?

Tap backtracked the trail a half mile or so, just to satisfy himself it came from the east, in the direction of the railhead at Stanholp. He went no further, figuring that the track probably would become obliterated by the great buffalo herd that also lay in that direction. Perhaps later he would ride around to the outer fringe of the herd and see if he could pick up the trail again. Then he put his horse into a trot and followed the trail out, toward its destination, until it hit the road a few miles from Demerest. There it turned in the direction of town but soon became lost in subsequent road traffic. Tap pushed Joshua on into Demerest.

Demerest was a typical frontier village. It consisted of one dusty, two-block long main street bordered by flimsy, false- fronted buildings. On both sides of the main road, one short block up, there was a back street mostly holding private houses, some still tent-roofed in canvas. Less than two years old, the town managed to survive on business that either flowed through to the Black Hills, had to do with hide taking or dealt with the fort. It was still small enough to worry about possible Indian attacks. Like many new towns in the territories, not all the business ventures were as reputable as they might be.

Demerest abounded with saloons and Tap stopped at the first one he came to--the Dakota Queen--and tied his horse. The saloon was on a corner lot on the left side of the road. On a hunch, Tap went around to the back street that ran behind the business houses on that side of the main road.

He walked down the two blocks that comprised the length of Demerest. Toward the end of the dirt backstreet, on the left side of the road, was a large pole-and-board corral. It was empty but Tap could see it had held a lot of animals not too long ago...and from the tracks, they were mules. On the right side of the road, hugging the back of a store that fronted the main street, was a small barn. The doors were secured with a padlock and hasp but there was a window on the side of the building. Tap wiped at the dust covering the pane and tried to make out the interior. It was too dark for him to see anything...not even the man inside standing back in a corner, watching him. Finally, after an attempt to force the door, Tap left and headed back for the saloon. Gunrunners were a high priority, but so was a beer.

The interior of the Dakota Queen measured about twenty-five by thirty feet. Its interior dark--the oil lamps were unlit despite the gloom--the room held a rough-hewn bar down most of the right side, a few tables and chairs scattered about, one gaming table at the back with a chuck-a-luck cage and, near mid-room, a stove warming a pot of coffee.

On the plain plank walls were a few faded prints of Civil War generals, one president who couldn't be identified through the crusting of dust and, over the bar, a large oil of a generously-proportioned woman, sans much clothing. Tap ordered a beer and when the barkeep brought it to him, the man spoke up. "Your handle's Tap, right?"

Tap gave a start. "Yeah! But how...?" He had been in Demerest only once. That had been when he went through, heading for McPherson...and this wasn't the bar where he'd

31

stopped. "I know you from somewhere?" Tap said.

"Wichita. About eight years ago. You were a deputy town marshall. You came into my place a time or two." The man wiped the bar with a rag, grinning. "Once stopped some would-be Texas hardcase from smashing my brand-new bar mirror, just in from Saint Louie." The man extended a hand. "Name's Ab Miller. Always meant to say 'thanks.'"

Tap shook Miller's hand with his right and downed the beer with his left. "That calls for another beer," Tap said, coming up for air.

"Coming right along," Miller said, filling the schooner again. "But this one's on the house."

Tap took the beer, this time sipping at it. "You own this place too?"

"Nope. Fallen on hard times. Just a bar jockey now. This place is owned by Deac Slater...like half the town is."

"Oh? Important sounding feller..."

"Important enough, I...excuse me." Ab Miller moved down to answer the beck of another customer and Tap bent over the bar and brought the schooner of beer to his lips again. The first beer was for guzzling. That spot within had been satisfied and now it was time to savor the brew. Tap was just bringing the glass down from his mouth when a voice from the back of the saloon sounded out. It came from a rear door Tap hadn't noticed in the gloomy little room.

"You! The tall jasper at the bar! What were you snooping around my place for?" It was more of an accusation than an inquiry.

Tap turned, slowly, putting the glass down, trying to let his right hand move casually from the beer to near his gunbutt. "Snooping...?"

"Yeah! Snooping! You was nosin' around my place, tryin' to get in."

"Sorry, friend." Tap kept his voice soft, trying to deflect the man's ire. "I'm new to the town...was just looking about."

"Like hell! That hen don't set!" The man moved out of the shadows, over to where the stove stood, about mid-room but nearer the far wall. "You were snooping! What for?" Who are you?" The man was nervous and quite agitated. He'd been left to guard something no one expected needed guarding. Now that someone had disturbed the status quo, he felt he had to take some action...however unwise.

"Look, I'm just passing through."

Tap had moved completely around to face the man. Doing so reminded him of his shoulder and he was damn glad it was his left that hurt, not his right. "I'm going to finish my beer and move on down the pike..."

"No you're not!" the man yelled. "You're stayin' here until my boss gets back!" Then he reached for the big Remington that was jammed into his waistband. A mistake.

The man was quick--quick but inept. He should have used the advantage of drawing first to take better aim. Instead, the shot went wide of Tap, almost hitting the bartender, ten feet away. Tap's first shot didn't do much better. The bullet struck the stove next to the man, spraying lead fragments at him, making him shy to one side. The next two shots came almost together--the man hitting Tap's half-full glass of beer and Tap taking the man just above the belt buckle.

Tap slowly walked across the room, his Colt cocked. It had all happened so fast that only now was his heart starting to catch up with events, beating hard and strong as it pushed the blood through him, making his temples pulse. He looked down at the man, laying against the stove, life dimming out of his eyes. Tap pushed the man over, away from the heat of the stove, and as he bent to get a better look at his face he heard the sounds of a pair of hammers clicking. Tap turned and looked over his shoulder to gaze down the barrels of an 8-bore Greener. "Just keep your hands where they be, mister," said a short, fat man with a tin star on his vest.

7

Ben Shipley was the town law. A short, beefy man in his late twenties, his main job was running Slater's Mercantile, a store at the other end of town, two blocks down from the Dakota Queen. A storeroom in the rear of the building was used as a 'jail' when needed. Shipley, accompanied by two other men, marched Tap down to the mercantile and through the front part of the store. This consisted of a long poorly lit room with counters on both sides.

The center of the floor was crowded with barrels of goods, tools and implements, creating a long 'island' that split the room into two long halves running front to back. Near the rear there was a wheelbarrow with a large sack of flour sitting in it that the men had to skirt around. Built over the center section that divided the room was a wooden rack, about six feet high. It extended from front to back and sloped toward the entrance. The rack was filled with heavy barrels, set on their sides. A wooden lever near the front of the rack, secured with a piece of rope, controlled a gate that allowed the barrels to roll down the ramp and be lifted off. The place smelled of onions, stale crackers and kerosene.

"In there!" Shipley barked, indicating a small room at the back. The four men moved into a room about twelve feet square.

"Sit!" Shipley said, pointing to a cane-backed chair and Tap dropped into it while the other two men lounged against the wall. Shipley himself took up station behind a small desk, placing Tap's gunbelt to one side on it.

"Ok, friend. Who you be?" Shipley's dark, black hair extended into a rough scrubble of three-day old beard. It gave his head the appearance of a cannonball on which someone had painted a face.

"Name's Tap Duncan. Army scout. Out of McPherson." Tap's reply was guarded but respectful. He saw no reason to rile these men...at least not yet.

"Oh? Not enough Indians to kill? Gotta come in and shoot up a few townfolks?"

35

Oh, oh, Tap thought. This wasn't going to go easy. "Seems to me, Marshall, that fellow was on the prod. He called me out and then pulled his gun. Ask your friend there," Tap looked to a hefty, hard-featured man on his right that Tap had heard Shipley call 'Jess.' "He was in the bar."

"And George said you were tryin' to get into the place he was lookin' after," said Jess, moving away from the wall slightly. "What were you doin,' tryin' to break into that building?"

"I think we best hold our scout here for the circuit judge to take care of when he comes by in a month or two," Shipley said. "I figure killing George Harper, after trying to break into the place he was watching, is a hanging offense."

Tap didn't like where this was going and he decided to do something about it. He launched himself from the chair, slamming into the desk and turning it and Shipley over. He grabbed his gunbelt as the marshall crashed to the floor, his feet in the air behind the desk. Jess, the man who had moved away from the wall, tried to catch Tap's arm as he broke for the door and Tap drove a fist into his midsection, doubling him over.

The other man, who had been to Tap's left and near the desk, came from behind, throwing his arms around Tap and wrestling him back to the center of the room. Tap lost his grip on the gunbelt and it fell to the floor. Tap dug in his heels and pushed back and heard the man grunt when he smashed into the wall, his hold on Tap broken. Tap's arms now free, he turned and swung a right into the man's face, staggering him and sending the man reeling into a corner.

Jess had regained his breath and came at Tap who weaved about, trying to get to the door. Finally Tap rushed forward, driving his head into Jess' belly and doubling him again when he hit the wall. Tap swiveled about, scooping up his gunbelt just as Shipley, who had gotten to his feet and mounted the overturned desk, came crashing down on him, driving Tap into the floor. A second later the other two men had joined in, raining kicks and blows at Tap who had no recourse but to curl up and protect as much soft territory as he could. Unfortunately, this left his shoulder wound exposed and a straight hit with a bootheel to his

36

back sent his mind into temporary oblivion. The last thing he could remember--dimly--was being yanked, toes dragging, down a hallway to be thrown into some dark recess of the building.

It was a little after nine when Ab Miller sauntered out of the Queen, his ten hour shift over. There was still a trace of pink in the sky from the sunset. Ab admired the beauty of it while he put his hands in the small of his back and threw his stomach forward. Twenty years of barkeeping, being on his feet ten or twelve hours a day, were taking its toll. Gonna have to get a clerking job, he thought. Something that required him to sit all day.

A noise to his right made him start and he saw a horse, pulling to the limits of its leather tie. It was trying to get at a watering trough set near the hitching rail but just a few feet too far away for the animal to reach. Thinking back, Ab remembered seeing the same horse when he took a short break around five o'clock. He stepped to the street and loosened the tether, allowing the horse to drink.

Ab looked the animal over, a big well-built dun. It was fitted with an army saddle, bridle and saddlebags. It even had a Spencer carbine strapped to it. But the horse didn't carry a 'U.S.' brand. Then it hit him. This was the scout's horse. It must have been there since its rider had entered the bar, almost ten hours before. Acting on impulse, Ab reached forward and checked the cinch for tightness. Then he stepped into the saddle and turned the horse around, pointing it down the road and out of town.

The knocking on the door woke Colonel Bruster with a start. He reached over, fumbled for a match and struck it, tilting his pocket watch to see what time it was. "Who in the name..?" He lit a nearby candle then scuffled for the slippers next to his bed and managed to slide a foot into one of them. He shuffled his feet a few more times, then, unable to find the second slipper, stood and shrugged into a robe that was on a nearby chair. Finally he went out into the hall and, one foot flapping, headed for the front door. When he reached it, he swung the door open with considerable vigor.

"There better be a good reason for this, Sergeant," he said as the light from the candle he carried fell on Sergeant Cook, that night's Sergeant of the Guard. "It's full twelve-fifteen in the morning!"

"Ye-yes sir," the sergeant said, not liking having to wake the commanding officer at this time of night any more than the colonel liked to be awakened. "Man here from town. Mister Miller. Says he needs to see you about Scout Duncan."

"Tap! Is it about Tap?" a feminine voice cried from somewhere back down the hall.

Bruster glanced over his shoulder to see his daughter, Matty, coming out of her bedroom, a wrapper pulled around her. "I don't know, yet...," he said, turning back to the sergeant. Behind the non-com he saw a new face catching the light. "You Mister Miller?"

"Yessir! Ab Miller," Ab answered and Bruster threw the door open and stepped back. "Best you come in, then. No need for the whole camp to hear this business."

Bruster moved into the little parlor that made up the front part of his quarters. He used the candle to light a lamp on a small writing desk and then took the chair behind it. "What's your story, Mister Miller? Something about one of my scouts?"

Ab stood, hat in hand while the sergeant remained by the door and Matty, her hand clutching the top of her robe, stood by her father, the worry showing in her eyes even in the dim lighting. "Yessir. Scout--name of Tap Duncan. Came into the Dakota Queen little before noon." Ab licked his lips. "That's where I work. Bartender. He was having a peaceful drink when one of the town toughs challenged him over something or other. Then the man, George Harper, went for a gun."

Matty gave a small gasp and Ab looked at her. "No need to worry, ma'am. Duncan didn't get a scratch. George though, he's being fitted for a pine suit." Ab looked back at Bruster. "Self defense, no doubt about it, but Ben Shipley, our town Marshall, tossed Duncan into the calaboose. Said he'd hold him there until the circuit judge comes by"

"And when might that be?" Bruster asked.

Ab shrugged. "Hard to say. Might be awhile. Usually, we have trouble, Shipley fines 'em, throws 'em into the tank a few days and lets 'em go." Ab ran the brim of his hat around with his fingers. This kind of business made him nervous. "If it's something big, like a shooting, he ships them over to Stanholp where the circuit court sets regular. Don't know why he's doing this to your scout."

"But Scout Duncan is all right?"

"Well, he's alive. I saw the two men who helped Shipley take him in. After they locked Duncan up they came back to the bar. Looked like they'd been in a tussle. I imagine your scout was on the receiving end as well as the delivering."

Bruster opened a desk drawer and pulled out three glasses. He reached behind him to a bottle on a small table and poured himself and the two men a drink, then replaced the bottle. Matty picked the bottle up and took a sip. Bruster knew it but pretended not to. He reached into the desk and removed an inkwell and a steel-tipped pen.

"Sergeant. Do you have a supernumerary tonight?" Bruster asked.

"Yes sir, Colonel. Corporal Higgins is our extra man for guard."

"Good. Have him hitch up my buggy and take Mister Miller to town. Then I'll have him deliver a little message to Marshall Shipley."

"Yes sir," the sergeant said, heading out the door. "I'll get right on it."

Miller cleared his throat. "If you don't mind, Colonel. Like to be dropped off just a bit outside of town. Wouldn't like certain elements of the place to know I was out here."

"No problem, Mister Miller. They'll never hear it from us."

Bruster continued to write. In his 'message' he laid out three items for Ben Shipley to consider. The first was that he, Colonel Bruster, would take full responsibility for the scout, Tap Duncan, and would see to it that said scout appeared at any court proceedings to follow. The second was that Demerest was a small town, still subject to Indian depredations. If the town expected the fort to come to its aid in the case of any such Indian attack, it would be well not to antagonize the commander of same. The third point was a thinly veiled suggestion that if

Duncan wasn't released, post haste, the 17th U.S. Cavalry itself might just come into Demerest and take the town apart.

It was a little after three o'clock in the morning when Corporal Higgins dropped Ab off and drove the buggy on to Ben Shipley's. The corporal's banging on the front door of the mercantile finally woke Shipley. He climbed down the rickety stairs that led from the little sleeping loft over the store. A candle in hand, he made his way through the aisles of barreled merchandise and counters stacked with soft goods. The candle flickered feebly and he banged his toe into a barrel of dried apples. He cursed roundly, as he hopped the last few feet to the door, his toe in one hand.

"What in the hell do you want?" Shipley yelled, opening the door and seeing the corporal.

"For you," the soldier said. "Compliments of colonel Bruster." The corporal turned and walked back over the porch to the buggy, stepping down into it.

"Hey! Wait a minute! What's this all...?" Shipley was too late. The corporal had already clicked the horse into motion and a second later was swallowed up by the dark of the Demerest street.

Shipley unfolded the paper and, in the candlelight, read Bruster's message. He swore again, under his breath, and stood there for a few moments in the cool night air, holding the paper and the candle in one hand and his foot in the other.

8

Shipley backed down.

"All right! Out with ya!" he said as the storeroom door swung open. Tap, lying against a couple of sacks of potatoes, raised his hands against the bright shaft of light that swept into the little storeroom, blinding him. Then two men moved in, grabbed Tap's arms and hustled him out of the storeroom and into the hallway where his eyes started to adjust to the light. He saw that the men were Jess and the other man Shipley had with him in the office the day before. Shipley walked ahead.

Tap, his head still full of cobwebs, was propelled from behind by Shipley's minions. He stumbled along the mercantile's aisles, through the big double front doors and out into the bright sun falling on the mercantile porch. Shipley, the Greener cradled in the crook of his arm, moved over to one side of the wide deck that fronted the mercantile building and served as a loading dock.

Standing easy near the hitching rail Tap saw a horse and a light, single-seated buggy. The buggy sat below the level of the dock and the top was up which prevented Tap from making out the driver. Tap looked at the sign above the store--SLATER'S MERCANTILE. Something occurred to him then, from the placement of the store on Demerest's main street. Close by the back of this building, perhaps directly behind, was the locked barn he'd tried to peer into.

"Here," Shipley said. He tossed something wrapped in butcher paper at Tap. Tap caught it and knew from the feel it was his gun and gunbelt. "Keep it wrapped until you clear town. We don't have that many citizens to spare."

Tap moved a hand across his sore ribs. "You're a hell of a lawman, Marshall." His voice was laced with sarcasm but Shipley missed it.

"I do the best I can to run a clean town," the marshal said, a touch of pride in his words.

"Yeah," Tap said with a shrug. "Nice evenhanded justice..." He didn't bother with the sarcasm this time.

Tap walked to the edge of the dock and stepped down into the buggy and then he stopped. "Matty! What the...?"

"Get in," she said, her voice low. "We can talk after we leave."

Tap stepped the rest of the way into the buggy and it bounced into motion, the movement reminding Tap just how stiff and sore he was. He slumped to one side in the seat and rested the back of his head against the little buggy's top support. The buggy had springs, front and rear, but he was still reminded of each ache and pain as it rumbled along. He looked at Matty. She was dressed in a dark skirt and hat along with a matching jacket that covered a white blouse already turning brown from the dust of the road.

Matty guided the horse out into the middle of the street and clucked the animal into a light trot that took them at a rapid gait past the false-fronted business houses. Tap glanced at the Dakota Queen as they neared it. There were two men standing out front. One waved but Tap didn't recognize either of them in the shade of the porch overhang.

When they cleared the edge of town Tap put a hand out to touch the reins. "Wait! My horse..."

"It's back at the fort. A Mister Miller rode it in last night. He's the one who told us about the trouble you were in."

"Miller...? Ab Miller? Man from the Dakota Queen...?"

"I guess," Matty said, reining the horse back into a fast, easy ground-gaining walk. "He woke us up...my father and me."

Tap sat back in the seat. Apparently he had friends he didn't even know about. He'd sure as hell make sure he bought that one a drink on his next visit to Demerest.

"Are you all right?" Matty said, her eyes anxiously searching his face, expecting to see some signs of a beating. "Mister Miller said they hit you..."

"A few bruises. Sore ribs," Tap said. "I'll live."

Matty ran a hand over his shoulder. "There's blood...!"

"Yeah. The arrow wound opened. Don't worry. Just dried blood. It's OK now." He tried to change the subject. "Why did Shipley let me go. The colonel have something to do with that?"

"Yes. My father wrote a letter to the marshall and said to let

42

you go." She was quiet for a few seconds. "I don't believe it was an overly friendly letter."

"Marshall Shipley isn't an overly friendly gent."

Tap gave Matty a querying look. "Your father let you come in for me? All alone?"

"No. He assigned an escort. Sergeant Quinn and a detail of men."

Tap stuck his head out of the buggy, looking about the landscape. "Well then...?"

"I told them I was leaving at one o'clock. I left at ten." Matty let a small smile cross her face. "I wanted some time to talk to you...alone. So I bribed the man on stable duty to look the other way while I drove out of the back of the holding pens, where I wouldn't be noticed."

Tap had to laugh at that.

"I expect," Matty went on, "that we'll run into them on the way back." She was quiet for a moment and then continued. "What happened the other day? In the saloon, I mean."

Tap stuck a foot up on the dashboard and leaned back into the seat. "Guess it isn't any secret that your father hauled me down here from Fort Rice to look for gunrunners. I saw some wagon tracks yesterday, out on the plains, when I was heading into town. Gave me reason to think that maybe it was someone hauling guns into Demerest." Tap gave a wave of his hand. "Long story short, I nosed around a few buildings, some hardcase took exception to it and braced me. He got off the first shot. I got off the one that counted. Self defense...but the town marshall had other ideas."

"My father gave his word you'd appear at court...whenever the circuit judge shows up."

"I wouldn't hold my breath. Shipley don't look like the type who wants too much outside law snooping around. In fact, the whole town of Demerest looks that way."

Tap decided to change the subject. "Enjoy your picnic?" he asked, and he felt the blood rush to his face in spite of himself. He was a little surprised to see a similar infusion of color creep up over the collar of Matty's blouse and into her face as she answered.

"Yes. Quite enjoyable. Of course, with the Indian trouble, we didn't ride far." She looked at Tap, her face still red but with a bit of defiance in her voice. "Did it bother you to see me with Captain Hawthorne?"

Tap hunched down in the seat, tilting his hat down to partly cover his face. "Some," he said, trying to sound nonchalant. "After what you said the day before..."

"Ten Years!" Matty cried, cutting Tap off. She'd turned toward him, her eyes bright with anger, her face now drained of its color. "That's how long I've waited for you, Tap Duncan!"

The heat of her words started Tap into a sitting straight-up position. "Why, I..." the words stumbled over his tongue.

"Over ten years! I waited for you, hoping you'd come back. That you'd write!"

"I wrote..."

"Yes! But fewer and fewer letters. All through the time father and I were stationed in South Carolina, in Washington, later in Missouri. Then, after eighteen sixty-eight, I never heard from you again. That was the last letter." Her voice had dropped down into an almost little-girl plea. "In the last one you said you were going to be living among the Cheyenne Indians for awhile. Trading. You never wrote again."

Tap was quiet, his head down, chin on chest. "I know. Maybe, partly...I figured if I were living with the tribes, I couldn't get a letter to you and I had a good excuse not to be writing."

"Then you don't love me anymore!" He words were low, breathless, without resonance.

"No," Tap said, quietly. "That's not true. It was because I loved you."

He moved further down into the seat again, as if he might be able to find refuge in it and disappear. He placed a foot back up on the dashboard and he looked out over the buffalo grass. It was just beginning to turn from its spring-rain greenery to a shade of gold. The smell of it, tinged with the dust kicked up from the buggy wheels, prickled his nose. He was not a man used to much conversation--even less so when it was directed toward himself and concerned women.

44

"When I was mustered out in Washington, in sixty-five, right after the big review, I tried to tell you how I felt." Tap made a face. "Guess I wasn't very good at it."

"I remember you said you had a chance to scout for the Eighteenth Infantry in Wyoming where they were going to build Fort Kearny. You said you hoped to save up enough money to come back and court me proper." Her voice held a note of exasperation, as if even at the time she had not felt it much of a reason to leave.

"That was part of why I left. You were a general's daughter and your family had money. I was a nineteen-year old half-wild kid who'd lived with the Indians more than the whites." Tap put a hand on Matty's arm and she closed her eyes and leaned into him.

"I couldn't ask for your father to bless our marriage when I had less than forty dollars in my poke. I figured, out west, there'd be chances to make a real stake. Enough so I could come back and ask for you, proper, not hat-in-hand."

Matty let go of the reins, letting the horse pick its own way down the road as she moved into Tap's arms. "Oh Tap!" she said and he could feel the light spread of warmth her tears made through his shirt. "Don't you know that never mattered? I've been in love with you ever since that day, in the camp near the Rapidan, when you rode up on a coal-black charger."

Matty smiled, wiped at her tears and then put her hand on Tap's shoulder. "You had just been ordered to scout for my father and you rode right up to his tent on this great stallion, pulling it to a stop and making it rear up on its hind legs."

Matty pushed herself away from Tap slightly, so she could look into his eyes. "And then you said--and I'll never forget the words--you said, 'General. I understand the Reb General, Kirkpatrick, burnt your home and stole your horses when he marched through the Valley in sixty-two. Well, last night I rode twenty miles south of here, fired his place and took this horse for you. That evens the score.'"

Matty put her head back down on Tap's chest. "Then you swung out of the saddle, put the reins in my father's hands...and noticed me for the first time. I'd been in my father's tent and just stepped out."

Matty laughed--a small clear sound that, to Tap, sounded like a little silver bell. "You looked at me, told my father you'd never seen anything as beautiful before, got all red and tripped over your feet when you turned to leave."

Matty sat up and again wiped at her eyes before taking the reins and moving back into the driver's position. "I said to myself right then, that was the man I wanted to marry."

"And I guess I thought you were the prettiest thing that ever stuck her head into a poke bonnet," Tap said, a little embarrassed in taking this look back at himself, to a time when he was not yet even twenty years old. "And those months we spent together...they were on my mind a lot of nights out there under the stars..." Tap made a little gathering motion in front of himself with his hands, as if to clutch the words he needed to explain how he felt. Finally he gave up.

"I can't really explain it so's you'd make sense of it. Man, he got his pride. I couldn't come to you penniless. But every time I made a little stake, something seemed to come along to wipe it out." He turned a hand over in a gesture of helplessness. "Finally, after a few years, guess I figured I'd never make my stake and you'd be better off without me."

"Is that really it?" she said, a sharpness now in her voice. "Those last few letters...they spoke less of us and more of the life you were leading. Are you sure that living like you were, among the Indians and the trappers and rowdies out west didn't mean more to you?"

"Maybe...some," Tap said, reflectively. "It could have been part of it too. Though not the past years. The buffalo being hunted into the ground. The tribes rounded up...it's all over...or soon will be."

"You feel at home with the Indians, don't you?"

Tap dipped his head. "Lived with them more than whites when I was a kid. My father was a trader. Ran a wagon to them tribes that was still wild but living on the edge of the white world. He'd leave me in a camp and take off for months at a time."

"And when you were older, an Indian maiden never caught

46

your eye?" Matty said, and Tap wasn't unawre of the the meaning she tried to keep out of the words.

"Saw some mighty pretty Indian women...and a few looked at me like they'd not be unhappy, I was to give some horses to their fathers." Tap shrugged. "Never did nothing about it, though."

"Is that what Indian's do? Buy their wives with horses?"

"Indian's don't buy their wives...not Sioux or Cheyenne at any rate." Tap leaned forward, resting his arms on his knees. "It's sort of a token. Horses are the most valuable thing the Indian owns. Giving horses to the woman's father, well, that's sort of like getting a white father's blessing. It shows the warrior realizes how important the woman is to the family."

Tap unwrapped the package Shipley had thrown to him and inspected his revolver. Then he started to load it. "It ain't necessary and it don't always happen--just like not every white couple what marries gets a blessing from a father--but it's the right way to do things. And if a woman doesn't want to marry the warrior, she don't have to." Tap put the now-loaded pistol in its scabbard on the floor. "Women have a say-so over who they marry. Anything they own before the marriage...or get later through trading or whatever, it belongs to them. They throw the buck out, they keep their plunder."

"Hmpf!" Matty said. "That's one improvement over the white man's world where a wife's property becomes the man's in marriage."

"Anyway, that's why I never came east again, to find you," Tap said. "I couldn't come with an empty poke...or lay claim to yours."

"But I don't care about that!" Matty said, exasperated. I want you, not your moneybelt!"

"And how do we live..."

"I have money. My mother left me..."

"Dammit, that's it! That's just what I'm talking about!" Tab pushed himself straight in the seat and crossed his arms in front of him. "I'm not gonna take money from..."

"Dammit yourself!" Matty shot back, so fiercely that Tap started. "Borrow the money from me! Start up a store. Or a

47

peddler's wagon, like your father." She turned on him, her eyes flashing. "You can pay me back--with interest. I love you Tap and you say you love me. That should take precedent over my money, your pride or whatever!"

Tap remained silent, his head bowed again, his eyes busy examining the creases in his knuckles while Matty went on. "I'm telling you now, Scout Duncan. I want you! I'm twenty-eight years old. I want a husband. A family." She slapped the reins for emphasis, causing the horse to break into a trot. "If you cannot come to see your way clear to ask me to marry you, I will have to consider another beau."

Tap didn't know what to say but his mind was racing along at a 2:40 gait, trying to come up with something. His efforts were halted by the sight of a dust cloud in the distance--down road. Tap quickly slipped the Colt out of the holster and checked the rounds again. Then he relaxed as he made out the blue of a uniform--and then another. It was Matty's 'escort,' lead by Sergeant Quinn, finally catching up with her.

Quinn and the half-dozen troopers with him pulled around, falling in on either side of the vehicle. Sergeant Quinn himself rode up and leaned down to look into the buggy. "Gave us a start there, Miss Bruster." His words were laced with concern. "Looked all over for you before we saw the buggy was gone."

"Yes. Well, I wanted to get on before the heat of the day," she said, airily. "I knew you'd catch up soon and what with all the patrols the colonel sends out, I didn't feel there was any danger." She gave the sergeant a dazzling smile and it seemed to work as he grinned weakly, saluted and dropped behind to join the men.

Tap didn't feel comfortable in leaving the conversation where it had ended. Still, he was grateful that the arrival of the soldiers had put the thing to rest...at least temporarily. When they reached the fort Matty pulled up at the headquarter's building and Tap helped her out of the buggy and onto the porch. She stood on tip-toe and gave him a very light, very quick kiss...on the cheek. Then her long skirt rustled across the porch to the door leading to the colonel's office. Just before going in she turned. "Think of what I said, my gallant scout," she said, her voice low. "And don't forget. There's the dance in a few days. I expect to see you there."

Tap drove the buggy around to the stables and turned the horse over to a trooper. Then he went and checked Joshua. While he fed the horse some oats, Sergeant Quinn walked up. "Hope that don't make me any trouble," he said. "Not gettin' out the same time as Miss Bruster, I mean."

Tap adjusted the feedbag under the horse's nose. "Oh, I think the colonel knows his daughter can be a bit contrary at times. Doubt if he'd blame you if she told you one thing and did another."

Quinn noticed the bruises on Tap's face. "Shipley rough you up?"

"Some."

"Well, to be expected. Town people and post people, don't always get along too well." Quinn emptied a cheek full of tobacco drainings into the dirt. "Towners, they figure what they do is their business and the military ain't got any call to interfere."

"Like running guns and rotgut whisky to the Sioux?"

"No, no! Nothin' like that! Just...civilians...they see things different than military. You steer clear of them, they steer clear of you "

"Yeah?" Tap said. "Well, I've got an idea I might steer in close to Brother Shipley again someday."

9

Tap kept busy the next few days, riding with routine patrols and staying away from the fort as much as possible. He didn't particularly want to run into Matty--though he was surprised to find how often she was on his mind--or the captain. However, there was no escaping the post ball, coming less than a week after his return from Demerest.

The ball was held in the enlisted men's mess, the single largest room on Fort McPhersen. The mess, located in the same row that contained the fort's administration buildings at the back of the parade ground, was decorated with flags and bunting. A temporary platform for the regimental band was built at one end of the room. Tables and chairs were arranged to provide a dance area and a place for food and refreshments. Outside, along the porch that extended across the front of the building, Japanese lanterns had been set out and lit.

By seven o'clock the festivities were in full swing. All the post officers and non-coms above the rank of corporal attended as did some invited townspeople. At the windows enlisted men looked in, enjoying the music if not the dancing. Occasionally one would slip around to a side window, behind the refreshment table, where an orderly would ladle punch into a messcup--that would usually already have a few splashes of exceedingly poor whisky in it. Just inside the entrance a soldier was detailed to take the cloaks of the ladies and put them on pegs set into the wall. Below these there was a second set of pegs so those officers who cared to tote their swords could hang them up.

There weren't many women--Matty, five other wives of officers or sergeants and a few that accompanied the civilians from town. All took turns in dancing with as many men as possible. In a few instances, when partners were lacking, a man would place a bandana on his arm and take the role of a female partner. Tap walked in just as a reel had finished and Matty, coming off the floor, rushed to his side. She wore a bottle-green dress--a lack of bustle showing it was a bit out of style--that exquisite tailoring had wedded to her body. The dress was daringly low-cut--at least for an army post. "Tap! Oh, I'm so glad you're here! Come! Give me a dance!" Without further ado she pulled him to the music, just starting again, and they swept around the floor.

"My," Tap said, looking down at her smiling face. "You are the bold one. Won't even let a man get a drink in his hand."

"It's only punch...unless you bribe the orderly. He's got a bottle under the table." She giggled. "I've already bribed him twice!"

"Brazen hussy!" Tap said, and whirled her about as the band went into a waltz.

Matty sought Tap out often...though not for every dance. She managed to be a partner at least once with almost all the men present. However, when it wasn't Tap it was usually Captain Hawthorne. The captain also made it a habit to cut in when Tap and Matty were dancing. Hawthorne made sure to give the scout a sharp look whenever he did so.

At one point Tap rested against the food table with a doctored glass of punch in his hand. He watched as Matty tirelessly swirled across the floor. To him, she looked stunning. Matty seemed to float in the arms of the young lieutenant she danced with. And seeing her in Hawthorne's arms bothered Tap more than he liked to admit.

Tap realized that the longing he'd felt for her in those late days of the war had returned full force. Still, the old fears lay heavy on him--what could he offer her? The captain, at least, would provide her with the kind of life--surround her with the same kinds of people--that she had always known. He tore his attention away from Matty when he noticed her father approach.

"Having a good time, my boy?" the colonel asked jovially, slapping Tap on the back. Over the years since the war the two men had served together several times and their relationship had always been a warm one. Tap somewhat assumed the position of the son Bruster never had.

"Fine, if your daughter doesn't dance my legs off, or," he made a face, "incite Captain Hawthorne into a fit over her dancing with me."

Bruster let out a short explosion of laughter. "Yes. We may

be building up to something there." He sipped from his cup and Tap could tell from the colonel's expression that he wasn't imbibing straight punch either. "He is quite taken with Matty," he went on, "and she is quite headstrong. We shall see...oh!" Bruster touched Tap's arm as a civilian approached, engaged in earnest conversation with Sergeant Quinn. "Here's someone I'd like you to meet. Deacon Slater? This is Tap Duncan, our new scout. Tap, Mister Slater...and you know Sergeant Quinn."

At the colonel's words the two men had broken off their talk. The sergeant nodded his head to all in general and quickly walked away, leaving the civilian facing Tap and Bruster.

"Mister Slater does all the contract freighting for the fort," the colonel said. "You may run across one of his outfits while you're out and about."

Slater was a tall man with a thin, creased face. A pair of thick, steel-rimmed glasses perched above a hawk nose. The hand he extended to Tap was cold and listless. To Tap, it seemed not from want of strength but, rather, as if in hopes that the touch might be as transitory as possible. "Pleased to meet you, Scout Duncan."

Tap returned the pleasantry and something clicked in his head--Slater. The same name he saw on the mercantile building where Shipley had kept him overnight--the man who the barkeep said owned half the town.

Slater's voice was deceptively soft. When he spoke he tended to push his shoulders up and stoop forward, like a gangly bird of prey. His hair was slicked back with some kind of grease and it was almost an iron-gray color. Tap pegged the man to be in his early forties. "Are you new to Fort McPherson, Scout Duncan?" he asked.

"Been here going on three weeks. Came from Rice."

"Ah! And are they also having unrest there on the upper Missouri?"

"Some, if you mean Indians. Tribes aren't too happy with the short beef rations and wormy flour they get from the agency." Tap tried to read Slater's face, to see if there was real concern there...or was this just polite chatter. But the man's eyes were gray as slate, as if to match his hair, and they revealed nothing. His face seemed an expressionless mask.

"Ah, yes," Slater said, nodding his whole upper body. "It would be a blessing if we could solve the problem. Running a freighting company, I am especially sensitive to any possible disruption by the hostiles."

Slater engaged Tap and the colonel in light conversation for a few moments more and then moved off. "Strange bird," Tap said, after Slater was out of earshot.

Bruster chuffed a short laugh. "He's from Saint Louis. Not at all happy out here on the frontier, but making too much money to leave."

"Where'd he pick up the 'Deacon' moniker?" Tap asked.

"Dunno. Think it's his real first name." Bruster grinned. "But he looks like a deacon, doesn't he?"

"Or a buzzard," said Tap, wryly.

Tap escorted Matty around the floor several more times but, around eleven o'clock, found himself out at the end of the porch. There were still a few enlisted men by the windows, listening to the music, and several NCO's taking in the cool night air. Overall, however, it was comparatively quiet, the band being at the far end of the building from where Tap stood. He was letting his mind wander--looking at the bright stars above--and he started all the more when someone suddenly grabbed his arm and spun him around.

"God damn it, I warned you, Duncan! I told you to stay clear of Miss Bruster!"

Hawthorne held on to Tap's arm, his fingers digging into the flesh and Tap had to literally shake himself free. "What's wrong with...? Hell, Captain! You're drunk!" Tap stood back to avoid the strong whisky smell coming from the officer.

"Not that drunk!" Hawthorne yelled and threw a right, his fist catching Tap, unguarded, high up on his left cheek.

Tap went sprawling off the porch. He dropped the two feet to the ground and stumbled backward until he hit the wall of the next building a few yards away. He pushed himself erect only to have to dodge another haymaker lofted by Hawthorne who had followed him off the porch. The captain, his punch unlanded, swung about and again came at Tap who caught both his arms

54

and heaved the man back several feet.

Hawthorne stood still for a few seconds, head down while Tap waited, fists balled up, not sure if he should just walk off or step in and paste the man one. Then Hawthorne made the decision for Tap. He reached down and drew the sword he was wearing.

Tap backed up a bit. Drunk or not, Hawthorne knew how to use the weapon. The captain advanced, point held low, forcing Tap out of the alleyway between the two buildings and toward the front porch railing. He lunged and Tap was able to jump aside. Hawthorne wheeled about and the sword hissed through the air in a broad arc, this time the blade just missing Tap by inches.

Tap could smell the fear-stink coming off his body. He was unarmed and had never--even in the war--faced a sword before. Hawthorne swept the blade around again and Tap caught the blow with his arm. The blade sliced through his coat and shirt and drew blood. Tap cursed under his breath and moved back. He tried to keep as much distance from Hawthorne as he could but was afraid to turn his back to make a run for it. A cavalry saber could easily separate his head from his body.

Hawthorne made a thrust and Tap was able to knock it away but the captain swung the blade back and jabbed him in the left shoulder, high up. Neither wound was causing Tap much pain yet but he could see that Hawthorne was warming to his task and starting to get in some serious sword work. Tap's face was now glistening with sweat despite the cool night air.

Then, from the darkness to his right, he heard his name called and he saw a flash--a glint--of moving light. Tap reached out and grasped the hilt of Whittiker's Bowie, thrown to him from the alley. There was sixteen inches of it, twelve of those being cold steel and razor sharp down nearly one half the top blade. This was a weapon Tap did know how to use. He reached over with his left hand to the porch railing and grabbed an army blouse someone had hung there. He draped it around his forearm with a quick swing while he continued to evade Hawthorne's sword. The two men made a small circular dance of their own to the music still coming from inside.

Hawthorne lunged again and Tap parried it with the Bowie, the clink of steel crystal clear in the crisp night air. The sword looked dangerous but the Bowie, its wide blade glistening in the light from the building, had a sinister, feral cast to it. With a sword, one could slash and pierce...but the Bowie was for disemboweling...

They touched steel several more times and then Hawthorne swung the sword again and Tap deflected the blade with his padded left arm. He noticed the captain was sobering up fast. Another thrust of the sword and Tap let it slide into the wrapped blouse. It missed Tap's arm but he didn't really care now. The blood lust was on him, driving out the fear, and he was perfectly willing to catch the blade between his arm bones, if necessary, to tie the weapon up and allow him to use the Bowie.

Tap yanked his arm to the side, the sword still entangled in the blouse, pulling Hawthorne to him. He slashed in with the Bowie, aiming straight for Hawthorne's stomach. The blade struck the captain full on his belt buckle. Tap tried to draw the blade up, into the man's soft parts but it snagged. It tore through cloth as half a dozen brass buttons flew into the air, sliced off by the big knife. Even in the dim light Tap could see that the fear he had felt only moments before now resided in Hawthorne's eyes.

Then there was a sudden bustle about both men as various sergeants, their attention caught by the action between the two, grabbed each around the elbows. In a twinkling they were dragging Tap and Hawthorne off in different directions and out of the gaze of higher authorities...as is the custom and duty of any sergeant worth his salt.

10

Tap was in Colonel Bruster's office early that next morning, his hat pulled down to shade the darkening bruise around his left eye. He was there to inform the colonel he would be gone from the fort for awhile, searching for sign of the gunrunners. For his part the colonel kept his head down, not looking at Tap as he granted his request. Tap was suspicious the older man was working hard to suppress his laughter. He wondered if the colonel realized how close he'd come to losing an officer—or a scout—or both.

It was around ten when Tap rode out of the fort on Jericho. It had been awhile since he had ridden the big gray and the horse's motion reminded him of the blow he'd taken from Hawthorne the night before--along with the general abuse he'd suffered in the past weeks. Today would be an easy ride. Tap would make a slow search for tracks, not be hell-bent to cover distance. He wore the Spencer over his shoulder, soldier style, the barrel stuck down through the carbine socket. At a walk it was a pretty comfortable way to carry the rifle and have it handy too.

Riding out of the camp, Tap thought back on the night past. He was glad the fight with Hawthorne had ended as it did. If he'd dropped the S.O.B.'s guts on the ground, like he tried his best to do, he thought, he'd either be in the stockade right now or making a dash for the Canadian border. He had to admit, it wasn't the previous bad blood between them or the blow Hawthorne delivered on the porch that had driven him. It was the fact that Hawthorne was a rival for Matty's affections. Complicating the situation was Tap's feeling that the captain might be the better choice for her.

Once clear of the fort, Tap headed for the herd he'd seen on his way to Demerest. It had moved on, further west, but Tap wanted to scout the eastern edge of the area it had occupied a few days before, toward Stanholp and the railhead. If the mule tracks he'd run across earlier had come from the railhead, there was a chance he could cut them on the far side of the herd. After several hours of searching Tap struck a trail...but it wasn't of mules. It was unshod horses, some pulling travois. The tracks were light so it meant they weren't loaded down--probably a hunting party just going out.

Looking for Indians wasn't what he was about right then so Tap wheeled his horse around, turning in the direction of Demerest. He had no intention of going near the town, though his thirst for a beer gave him pause. He slaked it--somewhat inadequately--with a drink from his canteen. The area to the west of Demerest was rocky and broken up, too much so for a large freight wagon to traverse and rough enough to shake apart a lighter vehicle. That meant pack animals--mules. Finding those might tell him as much as wagon tracks. If someone was running rifles out of the town, pack animals would be the way they'd go. Tap lined his horse out in that direction.

The most direct route to the west of the town took Tap over the ground where he had talked with the buffalo hunters. Nearing the killing grounds the wind, up to this time a gentle breeze bathing him in the sweet scent of the grass, became harder and brought him the foul stench of rotting meat. Tap topped a ridge and looked down on the open range below, now devoid of the huge herd but dotted with the sprawled out carcasses of thousands of buffalo, their hides pulled off, left to decay in the hot sun.

Though motionless in death the great animals appeared to still be writhing in their final agony. The glistening, skinless bodies seemed to pulsate in the shimmer of the heat waves boiling off the surface of the prairie. When he turned his horse toward them he saw the source of this illusion. Waves of carrion birds on the nearest carcasses arched their wings high above their heads. Then, with an awkward leap, they swept into the air and lumbered away in clumsy flight, guts full of putrid meat, to other corpses further on.

Tap felt a sickness. It was further inside him than just his stomach and more than could be accounted for by the smell...though that was bad enough. It was the waste--the wanton squandering of all this meat and what it was doing to the Plains Tribes. Their end as an independent peoples, a nation, was at stake. There was a time when Tap had seriously considered joining them in what some Indian leaders--Crazy Horse-Gall-Buffalo Lance--had envisioned--a fight to the finish against the whites. Tap had even once fought with the Cheyenne--undetected by the army--in an engagement against white troops, an act of treason if it had been discovered. In the final analysis though, he was a white man and in that direction his loyalties would finally lead him...influenced by the fact he knew that the Indians had not a prayer of ever winning.

The trail of the herd crossed the military road a dozen miles from Demerest. Here there were a half-hundred more dead buffalo, killed by townspeople who took the opportunity to come out and kill something. A few animals had some meat removed--principally that coveted delicacy, the buffalo tongue. But most putrefied under a hot, late-spring sun, intact with hide, horn and meat--robbed only of their life and purpose.

Tap rode on, cutting wide of the herd-path, crossing back and forth between it and the area to the north, toward where a line, pushed eastward, would come near the town...but no luck. There were tracks--disturbing since they looked like possible war parties--but all of unshod horses. Then Tap noticed a smudge in the sky, off to the south-west. He turned Jericho toward the smoke.

The wispy white tendrils grew stronger until they were just over the rise ahead and Tap pulled up. He wasn't sure what was causing the smoke but he wanted to check it out with care. About a week ago he'd been a prime candidate for feeding a fire himself. Tap tied his horse to a bush and unslung the Spencer, shoving it back into the socket attached to the rear of the saddle. Then he crept forward to the top of the rise. Once there he was able to look below and see what was making the smoke--half a dozen wagons, burned down to their running gear. Strewn about, not far from what was left of the wagons, were the bodies of nearly a dozen men. Tap went back and retrieved his horse and then walked down to where the bodies were.

The dead were scattered, haphazard, as if no real defense had been made. That surprised Tap. A dozen seasoned hide hunters with their big Sharps and Remingtons and some wagons to fight behind would make a formidable force. Whoever had caught these men unawares had been clever indeed. All the usable camp accouterments had been hauled off along with the hunter's guns, their horses--except two dead animals that Tap guessed were killed in the fight--and ammunition. Most of the bodies were still clothed. The attackers had drawn the line at taking the garments, permanently imprinted with the stink of the hider's trade. All had been scalped, however, and a few mutilated.

Tap walked around, studying the ground for sign when Jericho, ground-tied a few yards away, suddenly lifted his head. The animal stared off toward the ridge Tap had ridden down. Tap, alerted, moved toward the horse, reaching for the reins and the rifle but whatever Jericho smelled made him nervous and he side-stepped away. The hose trained to come at Tap's call, wasn't having any of it just then.

"Whoa!" Tap called, trying to be both firm and calming at the same time. "Hold it, boy." But the horse continued to shy.

Tap made another grab for the reins and the horse reared up on its hind feet. It half turned away from Tap and, when its forefeet hit the ground again, it snorted and trotted off, out of reach, its eyes rolled back to the whites. Then Tap looked to the ridge behind him and saw the line of Indians...and he recognized the one in the forefront. It was Buffalo Lance.

Tap swung around. Jericho was too far away to do him any good now, even if he would let himself be caught. The wagons were burnt so far down they couldn't provide cover. He pulled his .45 and made for the two dead horses, fallen close together and forming a rough 'V' shape. He hunkered down behind the horses--a poor barricade but it would have to do.

The line of Indians, about fifteen Tap guessed after a quick look, moved down slope. Then they split, an almost equal number of warriors sweeping around each side of him. Tap cocked the Colt but held his fire, not wanting to start the fight if there was any chance he might avoid bloodshed. No chance. A warrior on his left loosed an arrow at him and Tap snapped off a round. Both men missed but Tap's shot drove the rider wide. Tap heard the clap of a rifle from his right and felt the 'thunk' of the bullet hitting the dead horse. He saw a mounted warrior, sitting, reined up, about a hundred yards out. The man put his horse into motion while quickly reloading his rifle. Tap fired a shot--too quick--then held for a steadier bead and saw, somewhat to his surprise, the horse plow into the ground. The warrior fell free and was immediately picked up by another rider, the downed warrior jumping on behind his companion.

Tap was having to fight back the panic now. He was armed with only a pistol--a poor weapon against mounted men riding fast at a distance. While the horse carcasses provided him with some protection to his front, his back was exposed to anyone who wanted to stand out there and lob in arrows or lead. He heard the pounding of feet off to his far left and saw a mounted Indian coming at him full tilt, something--a war club?--held high. Tap raised himself to one knee, getting off two futile shots before the horseman was on him.

Tap felt a stinging blow on his head as the animal literally jumped over him, one hoof grazing his shoulder and knocking Tap back onto the dead horses. Tap got off one more shot at the Indian--his pistol was loaded with six rounds, the hammer carried between cartridge heads--before dropping the hammer on an empty. It was then he realized the 'club' had been a coup stick. The warrior had only been counting coup, to show his bravery. He could be depended upon to have a more deadly weapon next time.

Tap flipped open the Colt's loading gate and punched out the empties. Desperation gripped him and he looked around, trying to find Jericho, but the horse was nowhere in sight. Then he saw Buffalo Lance, coming at him from the rear of his barricade. The Sioux warrior had started less than a hundred yards out, his lance poised to drive home, his horse pushed to a full gallop.

Tap fumbled in a cartridge...then another and then gave up. He threw the rest of the shells he'd been holding to the ground and swung the pistol upward, hoping to get a bead on Buffalo Lance. Tap frantically clicked through the empty chambers, trying to bring up the live rounds in time to get an aimed shot off. But Buffalo Lance was mounted on his fastest war pony, bearing down hard, leaning partly over the side of his horse with the lance held low. Tap wasn't going to make it. Turned out, he didn't need to.

Both antagonists were so wrapped up in each other neither saw the horse that streaked in from Buffalo Lance's right, slamming into the side of his mount and almost knocking both horses to the ground only feet away from Tap. It was Horse Catcher.

The two mounted men took a few seconds to recover from the blow--indeed, the horses themselves stood nervous and shaking after they regained their footing. "No, Buffalo Lance," Horse Catcher said, slipping out of his war saddle and running a hand over his mount's neck, calming it. "Many Speaks is not our enemy."

Horse Catcher was dressed in only a breechclout. In one hand he carried a Sharps carbine. He was in his early thirties--a little older than Buffalo Lance--with a long, morose face that seemed to carry the sorrows of his race. "My heart was full of grief in our camp the other night," he said, directing his words to Buffalo Lance whose face continued to seethe with anger. "Still, Many Speaks is not our enemy,"

Horse Catcher turned toward Tap, extending his hand. "Will you forgive an old friend..."

Tap holstered his pistol and took the Indian's hand in his. "We have always been brothers," Tap said, keeping an eye on Buffalo Lance, just in case. "Because your heart felt bad one night, that doesn't change."

There was a series of 'yip-yips' and the three men saw, at the top of the ridge, another line of warriors moving down the slope. This one was headed up by Wolf Whistle, the band's chief. He was dressed in an old military coat and he didn't carry a weapon. Despite his being shot at, Tap was beginning to think this wasn't looking as much like a war party as he'd first thought.

"My brother," Wolf Whistle said, pulling his horse in next to Tap. "My heart is heavy that we almost killed you in our camp."

The chief put his hand out, his wrinkled face breaking into a smile when Tap clasped his forearm in a return gesture.

"We don't have 'white' brothers," called out Buffalo Lance, sitting nearby, his horse still dazed. "There are only 'The People.' All others are enemies."

"Not all whites are the same," Wolf Whistle said. "This one is our friend. It was Many Speaks who refused to lead Son of the Morning Star to the camp on the Washita because he knew it was a peaceful camp."

Tap looked at Buffalo Lance to see what affect these words had on the man. He himself well remembered later spending a night 'bucked and gagged' at Hawthorne's orders for his arguing with Custer against the attack. The warrior stared back, his eyes boring into Tap's. The scout wished he could see what was behind the brave's dark gaze. Finally Buffalo Lance kicked his horse into motion and moved a short ways away, standing off alone but close enough to hear what was said.

"These men," Tap said, sweeping his hand in the direction of the hider's bodies. "Did you kill them?"

"No," Wolf Whistle said. "We heard of this early today when one of our hunting parties found them. We came out to look."

"I would have done it," Buffalo Lance said, angrily, pulling his horse around and facing the others. "But it was done by an Oglala war party. Led by Crazy Horse."

Tap pricked up his ears. "Oglala! They've been hunting west of here these last summers. Why are they here with you Teton Sioux?"

Wolf Whistle started to answer but Buffalo Lance interrupted him. "I sent for them!" he said, striking his chest with his hand. "I have asked all the bands of 'The People' to council with me. The Cheyenne, too. So far, only Crazy Horse has come."

"Why?" Tap asked. "Bringing all those warriors together will only alarm the whites..."

"Good! If we band together, if we get more of the many-shoots...then maybe the White Chief in the east will listen to our words about his taking back the sacred Black Hills he promised us."

Tap looked around the half-circle of Sioux before him. At least a third sported repeating rifles, mostly '66 Winchesters and Spencers along with a few '73's and Henrys. The rest had various single-shots, both breechloaders and powder-and-ball.

Most of the repeaters looked new. Only the Spencer Buffalo Lance carried seemed older, its stock heavily decorated in an outline of brass tacks with more tacks making up a cross over the flat of the stock.

"You have good rifles," Tap said. "Where did you get them?" Wolf Whistle looked at Horse Catcher and Horse Catcher pursed his lips. "We get them from white men. We give them hides and pelts...and the yellow metal that makes the white-eyes crazy."

"Gold? Where do you get gold?"

"From our sacred places. Perhaps if we bring the yellow metal to the white-eyes, they will not need to go there."

Not likely, Tap thought. That will only spur them on.

Horse Catcher spoke again. "You should leave the blue-coats, Many Speaks. Go live in the big white men's village. Out here, there will be war. They attack our camps. Our land is overrun. The buffalo are killed by men who take only the hides, leaving the meat to rot." He shook his head, sadly, his long face more hang-dog than usual.

"Everywhere, throughout the different villages, there is talk of war. Go to your own lodge and live in peace. Out here," he swung his hand about, toward the dead hunters and the buffalo carcasses beyond, "there is death."

Tap looked to Wolf Whistle but the chief was silent. He was over fifty winters old and he could remember when he and his people roamed the land at will, not having to answer to anyone. Now they were hard-pressed to travel more than a day's ride without being challenged by whites claiming all the land as theirs.

"War would be bad for the soldiers, Horse Catcher," Tap said, "but it would be worse for you and your people." A warrior brought Jericho over to him and he took up the reins. "It's better to keep your young men walking the way of peace."

"HA!" Cried out Buffalo Lance. "The white-eyes don't know the ways of peace!" He wheeled his horse about in a circle, holding his lance high. "But I know the ways of war!"

He dug his heels into the sides of his horse and galloped off up the hill, the members of his society following him.

"It has been many moons since you sat in council with us, Many Speaks," Wolf Whistle said. "Would you join us tonight? I would hear what you have to say on this."

Tap thought about it for a few seconds. It wasn't likely anyone at the fort would panic about his not returning that night. "I'll come to your camp," He said. "I would be honored to sit and smoke with your wise men and chiefs."

It wasn't far to the Sioux camp but darkness had fallen by the time the camp had eaten fully of the fresh buffalo harvested from the passing herd. After, Wolf Whistle, the war chiefs and several older men retired to the chief's lodge. Tap was called in last and, as was the custom, went to the right after entering the tipi.

The interior was lit by a small fire near the center of the lodge. It cast fingers of yellow against the buffalo hide cone tapering to a small opening above. The air was heavy with the pungent aroma of wood smoke, animal fat, leather, dust, tobacco and man-sweat. To most whites the smell would have been noxious but Tap found it agreeable--comforting, even. It was a fragrance that was a mixture of those things close to the earth itself, the Mother that provided the Indian with all that he held dear.

Tap waited until Wolf Whistle invited him to sit at the guest's place, slightly behind Wolf Whistle, on the chief's left. He took the place, being careful not to step between the fire and anyone else in the lodge. Then Wolf Whistle brought out a pipe, filled it and, after taking a few puffs, passed it around to the others. Once it was returned, several warriors took out personal pipes and enjoyed them, including Tap whose curved meerschaum pipe drew considerable interest from the other men.

Wolf Whistle started the meeting by bringing up moving the band back to the reservation to live, as the government was pressing them to do. His words were quickly answered by Buffalo Lance, who wanted to fight the whites to the death. Then Horse Catcher spoke up and said he didn't mind living on reservations if the tribes could still move off to hunt. The two men then dominated the discussion. Each raised points to bolster their stand. Each received grunts from their respective followers

65

when the points were made.

Buffalo Lance wore no paint now. But, standing there, looming above the others in the confines of the lodge, the fire dancing shadow and light across his body, Tap thought that the warrior looked the manifestation of power. It was little wonder he had becoming the leader who might be able to unite the various bands into a fighting force big enough to challenge the army head on.

Finally Buffalo Lance had had enough of the talking. "Why should we give up our ways because these white dogs say we must?" he said the passion of his words gathering nods from men in the tipi.

"It will not be all that bad," Horse Catcher replied. "We will be given food and land. We won't have to worry about fighting other tribes...our women and children will be safer..."

"I like being a warrior!" Buffalo Lance threw back at him. "We are all warriors...or were when we were young men. We enjoy war. We enjoy the hunt. We like moving where we want to. Why should we give that up?"

"Because things change!" Horse Catcher said, tartly. He was beginning to lose his patience. "In my grandfather's time, we didn't have the spirit-dog. Then the Great Spirit sent it to us and things changed." He pointed with his finger to the tipi floor and then reached down and rubbed his thumb and the tips of his fingers together, the sign for 'earth.' "In those days, the world was ours. Now it belongs to the whites."

"No!" Buffalo Lance shouted. "I did not give the earth to the whites! The Great Spirit did not give it to them! If they wish it, let them fight us for it!" He continued to stand, his arms folded in front of him, his jaw clenched tight.

The tipi fell silent after Buffalo Lances' outburst. Wolf Whistle had not spoken for a while. Now he sat up and began. "I have been to the White Chief's lodge. To the east. Back when Red Cloud went, over five winters ago." Wolf Whistle took a puff of his pipe and slowly let it out. "I have seen the white man's villages. They would take as many days to walk around as there are people in our village. Their soldiers are as many as the leaves on the trees."

66

Wolf Whistle sighed. "If it were only me, I would fight, though I know it means death. I would sing my song and go to the Great Spirit with gladness in my heart for the years he let me live as one of 'The People.'" The chief shook his head, sadly. "But it is not myself I must think of. As chief, I must think of the women, the children, the old ones..."

The lodge was quiet for a few moments, only the sound of the crackling fire breaking the silence. Then Buffalo Lance spoke, this time his voice low and his words measured. "I had a dream not long ago." He extended his hands, left pointing to right, and tilted his head and then made the sign for 'sleep' and 'good.' Together, they made the sign for 'dream.' "I saw many white soldiers. They fell from the sky like raindrops. They landed among the hooves of my ponies and were crushed by them."

The Indian placed his hand, pointing down, over his heart and made the sign for glad. "I will be happy if the white soldiers are many because then I can kill more of them and gain great honor." Buffalo Lance looked about at the men still sitting on the lodge floor, then he sat back down himself.

Wolf Whistle looked at Tap. "Would my brother like to add his wisdom to this council?" he asked.

Tap cleared his throat. It was a great honor to be asked to speak in such a meeting and he tried to choose his words carefully. Like the others, he spoke in Sioux but often emphasized his words with sign. "If I were one of 'The People,' I would feel as Buffalo Lance. I would want to die as I had lived. As a free man--free to go wherever I wish."

Tap was quiet for a moment, then went on. "But the old life is over. You can fight my words but you cannot win. The question is, do you wish to destroy all your people with you or do you want to try to learn a new way, as your fathers did when the spirit-dog was given to you?" Tap held his left hand on edge, straddling it with the first two fingers of the right, the sign for 'horse.' "You will be a different people. You will learn new things. If the White Chief is fair with his children, it can be done, though it will be hard." Tap let the rest of his thoughts go unsaid--would the White Chief be fair?

The council finally broke up with no agreement reached--but Tap thought that was probably to the good. The two war chiefs weren't in agreement. Furthermore, Wolf Whistle, his words carrying considerable weight inside the tribe and out, was lukewarm to the idea of fighting. Peace might be maintained. If only, Tap thought, he could keep the repeating rifles out of the hands of the Sioux and Springfield rifles under Captain Hawthorne's command out of the Sioux camps.

11

The warriors left Wolf Whistle's lodge for their own tipis, Buffalo Lance still vehemently claiming that a war to the death was the only way for the Sioux to resolve their differences with the whites. When Tap ducked down to move through the tipi flap Wolf Whistle placed a hand on his arm. "This has been a good talk," he said, keeping his voice low. "Buffalo Lance can see that there are many who still feel a way other than war can be found. If he can't get many to follow him, then there will be no war."

"Hope you're right." Tap said, turning away. Then he stopped. "My brother. Will you tell me where your people are getting your many-shoots?"

Wolf Whistle looked at Tap in the glowing embers from the lowering fire. "There are men who bring them to us." His words were soft but they held a finality that told Tap he would learn no more from the chief's lips concerning the rifles.

Tap retired to a tipi, one of several set up for the bachelor warriors. It was a warm night and the sides of the lodge were rolled up to allow in a light breeze. He found an unoccupied buffalo robe to lie on and covered himself with a light blanket that one of Wolf Whistle's wives had given him.

Somewhere near dawn Tap awoke, realizing he wasn't alone in the buffalo robe--it was loaded with lice. Itching and scratching, Tap headed for a small stream behind the camp.

He was getting soft, Tap thought. Lice were a fact of life among people who didn't have the luxury of convenient laundry and bathing facilities. In the past, he'd just learned to live with it. Now it bothered him. In the breaking light of a morning sun Tap found some plants that he'd seen Indian women use as soap. He bathed in a small pool, washing his body and scrubbing his clothes with the plant roots. Then, shivering in the cool morning air, he walked naked to a small campfire, off to one side of a lodge. It had broken back into flame from the night before. Tap arranged some cooking sticks to hold his clothes and, as they dried, he stood by the fire, soaking up its heat.

Tap had been standing there for about a half hour, near asleep on his feet in the fire's warmth, when he was startled by a voice. "Well, white man! Do you always come naked to your breakfast and cook your clothes to eat?" Tap swung around to see a wrinkled old woman, just come out of the tipi, standing there with a small kettle in her hand.

Flustered, he grabbed his longjohns and covered his private parts with them, grouping for the Sioux words he wasn't able to come up with handily. "Little mother! I was trying to dry my clothes...I wasn't cooking, I was..." He stumbled around, trying to climb into his half-dry underwear.

"Don't bother," the old woman said with a coarse laugh, waving off his efforts. "I've had three husbands in my time. At least two of them would shame you." She walked over to some large buckskin bags and rummaged around for food. "But, " she added, "if you stand around like that long enough, I'm sure some of our young maidens might be willing to move into your lodge and cook and wash for you." She cackled again and Tap, red-faced, finished putting on his damp clothing and went for his horse.

He'd staked Jericho near the camp the night before, not trusting him to stay with the Indian ponies. Returning to the circle of tipis with the horse he saw a young man step out of a bachelor tipi not far from the one he'd occupied. The man stared at Tap for a moment and then ducked back into the tipi with considerable haste. Tap wondered at the man's action and then realized he'd seen him before. It was the same Indian Sergeant Quinn had been talking with by the horse pens at the fort. Apparently the man was more than just a 'blanket' Indian.

After saddling Jericho, Tap stopped by Wolf Whistle's lodge to say goodbye. He stressed the need to keep the young men in the tribe off the warpath. The old chief agreed but Tap knew there was only so much Wolf Whistle could do. He was chief of his band, not king. The warriors were individuals and could pretty much do as they pleased.

Tap was still a good three hours from McPherson, and probably two hours out of Demerest, when he topped a ridge and rode smack into a herd of mules, all carrying empty packs. He

70

pulled up as the seven men pushing the two-dozen or so animals rode around to confront him. He was surprised when the one who stopped closest to him turned out to be Deacon Slater.

"Well, good morning, Scout Duncan. Didn't think there were any patrols out this way today." His high voice carried an edge and Tap noticed that everyone had drawn a rifle from a scabbard and now rested it across their saddles...except a moon-faced youth in a derby hat who stood his horse to Slater's right. He had his weight shifted in the saddle so that the big Smith & Wesson .44 on his hip was very near the hand that rested on his waist, holding his coat back. Another kid who's a would-be badman, Tap thought, and trying mightily to convince everyone of it.

"No patrol," Tap said, evenly. "Just doing a little looking around. Been a heap of years since I last scouted through this country. Getting reacquainted." He nodded toward the mules, trying to sound casual. "Quite a bunch of brayers you got there. Most freighters haul with bullocks."

"Of course. Of course," Slater said smoothly. "I use them too. Depends on what we're moving. Heavy stuff--freight--oxen do fine. Need to move things along, mules or horses are best." Slater tried to smile but it didn't really work on that long, pinched face. "Got to give the government whatever service they require."

Slater looked back at the mules and then around to Tap. He felt he had to offer some explanation for the animals being there and he laughed again and said, "Had this bunch pastured out away from town, getting some new grass. Indians came along and spooked them." He took off his white planter's hat, wiping his brow, and gestured toward the mules with it. "Just now getting through rounding them all up again."

Tap knew he should have left it at that and moved along, but he couldn't resist asking one question; "You usually pasture them out with their packs on?"

Slater's expression still held the half-grimace that passed for a smile but it changed, ever so slightly. The man with the derby moved his hand down slightly and an alarm went off in Tap's head. He moved his own right hand, as casually as he could, away from the pommel of the McClellen and to his right hip. The move wasn't missed by Derby. "You seem to take an awful big interest in things that ain't none of your business, friend," Derby said.

"No harm meant," Tap said, feeling the hairs at the back of his neck prickle. He probably could dump Derby out of the saddle, but he'd play hell trying to get the rest of them, especially since there were more of them than he had cartridges in his Colt. "Sometimes my mouth is bigger than my good sense."

Slater broke the tension, moving his horse away and to Tap's right. "Well, no matter. We need to get these animals back." He continued out to the point, at the head of the mules, while the rest of the men tailed off to the sides and rear of the animals...all except Derby Hat who held his horse still for a few more moments.

"You get in to Demerest, be sure and look me up, ya' hear?" he said, his hand now only an inch from his gunbutt.

Tap nodded. "Be pleased to," he said, dryly.

His hand still held in place, his position unchanged, Derby Hat moved his horse forward, toward the others, now several hundred yards off across the prairie. He held his pose and his gaze on Tap until almost back to the herd. Then he turned away and spurred his horse ahead.

Yeah, Hardcase, Tap thought. Maybe I'll just take you up on that offer.

It was nearly noon when Tap rode out of a line of trees near McPherson and saw a pair of riders moving toward the fort. Even from a quarter mile away he could tell it was Matty and Hawthorne. He tightened his jaw and pulled Jericho up, waiting long enough for them to gain the fort, put their mounts away and clear out of the stable area. Then he nudged Jericho forward. Once at the stable he saw the soldier on duty taking care of the two horses. Tap unsaddled Jericho, gave him a rubdown and put him in the shed so he could eat a ration of oats without having to fight the other horses for it. When he turned to close the stable door he bumped into Matty.

"Matty! I didn't see you..."

"Are you all right?" she asked, concern in her voice. Then she touched his shirt. "You smell like...smoke...?" she said, catching the scents of the drying fire from the previous night.

"Long story. Happened in an Indian camp."

"You were in an Indian camp?" she said, her tone bordering on panic. "Did they try to burn you at the stake again?"

"No. Nothing like that. Friendly visit."

"You didn't return last night..."

"Suppose that's what the captain and you were doing...out searching for me." The words were laced with sarcasm and Tap was a bit ashamed at having voiced them...and yet he was secretly pleased at the shocked look they rendered from Matty.

"I...I always go for a morning ride..."

"Several hundred men on this post. Don't suppose any other of them can escort you..."

Matty flushed red, then swiftly turned and started away. Tap grabbed her arm, holding her back. "You're trying to make me jealous! Admit it!"

"No! Yes! I mean..." She pulled against Tap's grasp a moment more and then relaxed. She put a hand to her face as she lowered it, preventing him from looking into her eyes. "I told you. I want you to decide if you want to begin where we left off...after the war. If my being with Captain Hawthorne helps you to make that decision," Matty looked at him, her eyes now flashing, "all well and good. You can either declare your intentions to my father and ask for my hand," she stiffened her back and squared her shoulders, "or stand aside and let me become an officer's wife. You know which one I prefer."

Tap released his grip and Matty turned and walked from under the stable overhang. Then she put a hand on an overhang upright, half turning back to Tap. "Now, you decide which one you prefer." Matty turned abruptly and disappeared around the building.

Tap stepped, grumbling to himself, into the scout's quarters where Whittiker was just pulling on a pair of boots. "Hey, old son. You stink like an Injun!"

"Oh, shut up!" Tap said, going to his bed and taking a carpetbag down off a shelf.

"My, my! Been talkin' to Miss Bruster, have we?" the old man chuckled.

"No I haven't been...! What the hell is this? Since when have you become such an expert on women?" Tap threw the bag on his bed and started rummaging around in it. "You've never even been married!"

"Have too! Back in twenty-six." Whittiker's expression changed, his voice no longer jovial. "Manden woman. Died of the fever five years later." The remembering of it softened his tone. "No need to get yer shirt all starched up."

"Sorry..." Tap noticed the old scout's bed covers were still pulled back. He wanted to change the subject so he said, "You just getting up?

"Yeah. Long scout yesterday. Up 'round Douglas Creek. Ran into a trail Lieutenant Grimes wanted to keep to. Tried to tell him it didn't look like hostile but he was on the scent." Whittiker yawned. "Kept us in the saddle most all night."

"And?"

"Crows. Friendly. Out tryin' to pick up some Sioux horses. We got in around five in the mornin.'"

"You should have been scouting west of here, other side of Demerest."

Whittiker's eyebrows shot up. "Why?"

"Saw that fellow, Slater. From town. Early today he was leading a string of pack mules back from somewheres." Tap sat on his bed and began pulling stuff from the bag. "I spent the night in Wolf Whistle's camp..."

"That explains yer smell."

"Yeah...well short of it is, ran into Buffalo Lance and Wolf Whistle out on the plains. Wasn't for Horse Catcher, my hair would be swinging on Buffalo Lance's belt today. Anyway, camp had a passel of repeaters in it. Nobody was talking but I'm betting Slater's been making deliveries."

"We got patrols out to beat hell. How come we never seem to run into them fellers?"

"Dunno. By the way, you do any scouting to the west of the military road and about ten miles south of Demerest, you'll run into a bunch of hide hunters."

74

"Heard there was an outfit chasing that big bunch a buff went through here t'other day. Them?"

"Yeah, but now they're laying out on the grass, keeping the skinned buff carcasses company."

"Buffalo Lance?"

"Nope. War party led by Crazy Horse."

Whittiker's eyebrows almost shot off his head. "Crazy Horse? What in tucket...! What's he doin' around here?"

"Buffalo Lance. He's trying to get the different society chiefs to band together. Wants one last war against the whites. Even if it drags the whole Sioux Nation down with it."

Tap stood, in his shirtsleeves, and strapped a shoulder holster over his left shoulder. "Right now, Wolf Whistle, Horse Catcher and some of the more reasonable men are keeping the lid on. But if officers like Hawthorne and Grimes keeping pushing hard, and if repeaters keep getting into the tribes..." He shrugged.

"What's that all about?" Whittiker said, pointing to the small holster now hanging off Tap's left shoulder, concealed by the coat he'd put back on. "Gonna do a little socializin'?"

Tap pulled out the shoulder gun, his old Colt Navy that, after the new .45s' were issued, he had cut down to three inches and converted to take .38 cartridges. "Slater seems to be a model citizen, way the colonel talked of him at the ball. No use accusing him of anything until I've got some real proof. Figure, might be some in a certain barn I know of in Demerest. Think maybe, tonight, I'll go look it over."

"Want some company?"

"Could come in handy. Welcome to tag along—if you've got enough beauty sleep."

"Good!" the old man said, grinning. "Give me a chance to take 'Ol' Percy' here out fer an airin'." He reached back to the gunrack behind his bed and lifted out a tremendous, heavy double-barreled shotgun.

"Holy... Where did you get that cannon?" Tap said taking the huge four-bore muzzle-loader from the old scout's hands. "This thing must weight twenty-five pounds!"

"Bought 'er off a feller passin' through town a week ago. Market gun. Used by commercial hunters fer takin' lots a birds at once. Feller was down on his luck and had three of them guns. I bought that one."

"The bore on this thing is more than an inch across," Tap said, shoving his thumb into one tube. "It must sound like an artillery piece when it goes off."

"Oughta. Each side throws a quarter-pound ball. 'Cept, I load 'er with buck, birdshot, nails. Whatever's handy."

"Well, bring it along," Tap said. "Might help even up the odds a mite."

12

It was just after dark when the two scouts rode into the outskirts of town, Tap mounted on Joshua. They pulled up easy on the opposite side of the street from the Dakota Queen. They sat there for a moment, part way up the side street leading to the second back road that ran parallel to Demerest's main thoroughfare.

"Where's this here barn?"

"Down near the end of the other back street. Behind Slater's store, I think. Let's mosey by."

The two men crossed the main road and swung into the back street that started behind the Dakota Queen and ran down to the barn that held Tap's interest. When they neared the place, Tap nodded his head. "That's the place," he said, pointing to the small barn opposite the livestock pen--still standing empty. Apparently Slator had put the mules elsewhere.

"Barn's dark. But there's a light up there." Whittiker pointed to a small window high in the building that shouldered up to one side of the barn.

"That's Slater's mercantile store. Think Shipley lives in that room. Need to get him out." Tap was quiet for a few moments. "Got me an idea."

Tap pulled something out of a piece of canvas tarp tied behind his saddle--a short, stout piece of metal. "Crowbar. Try not to lose it. Borrowed it from the post carpenter. I'm gonna go down to the 'Queen. I think, me showing up, somebody'll let Shipley know and he'll come running. If the light goes out, or you can hear him leave, tear the hasp off that door and see what you can find. Got matches?"

"Yep."

"OK. I'll tie up across the street from the saloon. When you get done looking around, come by. I might need your help."

"'Least, this time, you won't be tied to a stake."

Ab Miller should have been off shift by this time--almost nine-thirty. However a night barkeep had a sick wife and Ab was filling in for a few hours. It was a normal week-night crowd. There were drinkers, card players, a few suckers at the chuck-a-luck table and the occasional customer taking a bargirl to the rooms on the second floor, accessed by a stairway set in a back corner. The place smelled of a day's worth of cigar smoke, stale spilled beer and sawdust...and kerosene, now that night had fallen. Ab had just finished polishing a row of glasses when he glanced up and saw a familiar--if unexpected--face push through the bat-wing doors.

"Hello, Ab," Tap called out. "Pour me a beer...and one for yourself."

"Duncan!" Ab said. "Last person I'da thought..." He reached for a couple of clean glasses. "Taking a chance coming in here, ain't you...after what happened?"

"Can't see myself letting the likes of Shipley getting between me and a beer. Anyway, I wanted to thank you proper for bringing my horse back and letting the colonel know..."

"Hey! Shoosh!" Ab said. He half-raised a hand in a gesture of silence and looked around the bar, worried Tap's words may have been overheard. "Keep that mum."

Tap dropped his voice and leaned over the bar, his beer in hand. "Sorry."

He looked into the bar mirror and was gratified to see a man quickly leave a table near the back and, his eyes on Tap, head for the front door.

"I forgot you said Slater owns most of this town," Tap said, shifting his attention back to Ab.

"Including Marshall Shipley. Best a man makes himself to look neutral, he ain't an actual bootlicker like Shipley."

"Well, thanks anyway." Tap looked toward the door. "Be truthful, I'm expecting the marshall to show anytime now. If something gets started, just stay out of it." Tap took a long drought of his brew. "No need for you to mark yourself."

"You can get beer at the fort. Just why are you here?"

Tap kept his voice low and briefly outlined his efforts to find some trace of gunrunners in the area, touching on his meeting of Slater out on the prairie. "I need to find some hard evidence that Slater is wrapped up in this. If he is, then hauling him in to a federal court ought to cut down the gun traffic considerable."

Tap pulled two dimes from his pocket and laid them on the counter to cover the beers. "Right now, friend of mine is down at the barn behind the mercantile. As soon as Shipley freights clear of his room, he's going to bust in and look about. So I expect..."

Tap's words were cut off by Ab's head jerking up, his eyes moving toward the front door.

Tap turned around, slow. The mirror behind the bar hadn't been long enough to allow him a view of the door. He put his back to the bar and rested there, easy, a slight smile on his face. This was working out fine.

Shipley, the Greener in his hands, moved away from the batwings and toward the middle of the room. Jess was close behind and he sidled to Tap's left, stopping near the end of the bar, about ten feet away. He had a Remington Breech-loading rifle in his hand. There was an open section of side wall between the bar's end and the front inside wall. It held a window, propped open with a stick to allow in air. Jess leaned back against the wall next to the window, his right elbow on the bar. He grinned at Tap.

Tap remembered the back door and he looked toward it just as the moon-faced kid with the derby hat came through, the Smith in open display. Tap noted where the little gunman took root and then swung his eyes back to Shipley. The player with a scattergun in his hands was usually carrying the most dangerous cards in a game. And to most of the patrons in the bar, a game it was, one they wanted to see. A few souls, wise in the ways of what can happen in a frontier saloon when guns are displayed, hastily left by the batwings. The rest moved toward the back by the chuck-a-luck table. It was a slow night and a diversion would be welcome.

Then Shipley called out, "Will. Come on in. We got him wrapped up."

When 'Will' stepped through the batwings, Tap recognized him as the third man who had given him the beating in the marshall's office the week before. A big, clean shaven man with a permanent determined-look set to his jaw, Will stationed himself in front of the batwing doors, a big, double-action Starr revolver shoved into his wristband.

"Barkeep!" Shipley said. "Pull this feller's fangs and shove it down bar."

Ab looked at Tap who turned his head sideways and spoke low. "Do it. I've got a stingy."

Ab reached down, pulled the Colt out of its holster and, at Jess's beckon, slid the gun down the bar to him. Jess picked up the gun, laughed and then returned to supporting the wall. Tap leaned back against the bar, his arms folded, relaxed. The loss of his gun and his softened stance seemed to put his captors at some ease too...except one man.

"Give him back his gun, Ben," Derby Hat said, using the ball of his hand to polish the backstrap of the Smith. "This here is Tap Duncan. Famous scout. Famous pistolero." He let out a short, mocking laugh. "Man here, at the Battle of Dead Horse Wells, he almost shot up every buscadero in Sonora."

Shipley looked at Tap, his eyes a bit bigger. "You that Tap Duncan?"

Tap cursed under his breath. The story of that shootout, years before, followed him everywhere he went. "Yeah, but don't take such stock in your friend here. That story gets better and better every time it's told. I was with three other men in that fracas and they totaled up most of the score."

"Give him back his gun, Ben," the man repeated. "I want a' try him."

"I'm the law here, Griff," Shipley said, his voice sharp. "You get back to tendin' Slater's affairs. I'll take care of this."

Griff looked crestfallen and he took his hat off and swung in against his leg. The derby had hidden a shock of sandy hair that, with his round face, accentuated the youthfulness of his features. Tap guessed he wasn't more than nineteen or twenty years old. "Come on, Ben! This goes back to out there. Out on the grass..." He indicated the prairie with his hat. "We had words..."

"Out!"

Griff shot one last look at Tap and then turned and went through the rear door, stomping his feet...like a kid, thought Tap. A dangerous one. A kid with a gun could be impetuous, unpredictable...and their reflexes lightening fast. Maybe he owed Shipley one, his sending Griff on his way.

Tap was brought back around by Shipley calling his name. "Duncan. I thought I told you to stay clear of Demerest."

"Just wanted to put your mind at ease, Marshall. Show you I was still around." Tap's voice was slightly mocking. "Thought you'd be happy, knowing I wasn't making a run for Canada."

Shipley made a movement with his shotgun. "Well, you was wrong. Now you can make another visit to my storeroom. You know the way."

"Wait a minute!" Tap pushed himself away from the bar, his hands at his side. "You can't arrest me for no reason..."

"My town, I can arrest you for havin' blue eyes. Now get movin.' I think Jess and Will want to have another 'talk' with you before we lock you up for a few days." Shipley spat into the sawdust on the floor. "And I don't care what kind of snotty letter your Colonel writes. You can damn well stay put until I feel like letting you out."

Will was bringing his revolver up to join the scattergun pointed at Tap when thirty-six inches of double barrel, four gauge shotgun shoved itself into the room through the window in the side wall. When Whittiker touched off the right barrel a one-foot wide hole appeared in the opposite wall, followed by a thunderclap and a dense cloud of dirty white smoke that nearly filled the front part of the bar.

"Hold 'er right there, Marshall," Whittiker yelled from outside the window. "The next load separates yer gizzard from yer collarbone."

Both Will and Shipley had been frozen in place by the force of the explosion. Indeed, so were most of the saloon patrons. Now Jess changed that. Whittiker hadn't noticed him standing just to the right of the open window and he didn't see Jess knock away the stick propping the window open. The sill crashed down and threw the barrels up setting the great gun off again. Upstairs a woman screamed as the load of shot hit the bottom of the thundermug she'd been using. The porcelain facility, blasted to smithereens, literally saved her ass. The spectators on the main floor were galvanized into action and in their mad dash for the batwings, swept Shipley and Will along with them.

Tap moved forward, toward Jess who stayed by the window but raised Tap's .45 and snapped off a shot. Tap had already pulled the Navy and he thumbed off three quick shots, two making it into Jess. They took him high up in the right shoulder and rammed him back into the wall. None were necessarily fatal but he was out of the fight. Tap grabbed the .45 with his left hand as Jess slid down the wall, his eyes already dimming out.

Ab was still behind the bar and he yelled, "Back door! Take the back door!" and Tap broke for it since everyone else had headed for the front door--or the window on the far wall. Tap made it out the door and started to turn left, to get around the saloon and to his horse across the street. Then two shots blazed from out of somewhere in that direction and Tap heard the voice of Griff yelling, "Pull your gun, Duncan! Let's see how much sand you've got!"

Tap snapped off two quick shots from the Navy and headed down the back street, in the direction of the mule pens and the barn, two blocks away. He tried to keep to the cover of the buildings on his right while several more shots came from Griff's gun.

Tap fired again when he got to the street that divided Demerest into two blocks and then ducked down it, heading for the main road. He holstered the empty Navy--reluctantly--and switched the .45 to his right hand. A better weapon, maybe, but he had used the Navy for over ten years and was a good shot with it.

When he reached the main street, Tap looked to his right, back up to the 'Queen, a block away. Men were milling around out front and he wondered where Whittiker was. He couldn't see his horse hitched across the street from the saloon. He guessed-- hoped--that the old scout had moved the two animals around to the other back street.

Tap ran across the road, intending to continue down the cross street. However, several shots came from that quarter and drove him to his right and up on the wooden walk in front of the business houses on the left side of the road. He fired several shots toward the side street and stumbled along, coming into the glow of four Japanese lanterns set out in front of a saloon named

82

'The Oriental.' A narrow alleyway ran toward the back street from the edge of the saloon and Tap started to head for it.

"There he is!" someone shouted. "In front of the Oriental!" Bullets began to seek him out, slapping into the wooden sidewalk and the clapboard siding of the buildings behind him. Desperate, Tap stopped his run for the alley and dove off the wooden walkway and into the street, getting a mouthful of dirt and a skinned up leg before taking refuge behind a watering trough and the shadow of the hitching rail. He heard the shots thudding into the trough and knew that he couldn't stay there. Once the water drained out bullets would start making it through both sides.

Tap reloaded the empty chambers of the .45 and stuck his head up over the trough. His heart was pounding in his throat and he spat out the dust he'd picked up diving to the ground. In the light from the lanterns someone picked out his movements and there came more shouts and several guns opened up on him again.

Tap didn't even bother to throw a shot back. The lights above made his movements too visible. Then he heard a shout from down street, on his side of the road. "Get ready to run!" yelled Whittiker.

Tap raised his head enough to dimly make out the old man, several hundred feet down the boardwalk, standing in the back of a wagon. He had the huge shotgun pointed his way, but high, and when the thing went off, the four lanterns, taken in flank, shattered apart, plunging the area into darkness. Tap, fear giving flight to his heels, was up in an instant. He ran for the edge of the Oriental and careened down the narrow passageway between the buildings, his pistol ready in case it held an enemy. It didn't.

An instant later he was out on the back street and he looked to his right. Relief swept over him at the sight of two horses. They were down near the end of the street, silhouetted against the night sky and fidgeting at the sound of the shooting. Tap ran toward them, giving out a little chirping whistle that was answered by a nicker from Joshua. Tap grabbed the reins and a second later Whittiker was beside him, swinging his lanky frame up into the saddle, spitting a couple caps out and into his hand

and then shoving them onto the nipples of the big four-bore. "Fool's errand! he said. "Nothin' in that barn but an old dougherty ambulance with built-up sides!"

"Ain't the time for jabber! Let's make tracks!"

"All right! Then head fer the road," Whittiker said, but Tap held up.

"That takes us right by the 'Queen. What about Shipley?"

"Ol' Percy here can take care o' that!" said Whittiker, pulling his horse around and sending the animal down the back street, around the corner and toward the next corner and the Dakota Queen.

At the sound of the horse's hooves a few shots started ticking around them from that direction. Tap flipped off a few rounds in the general direction of the saloon, but high, not wanting to kill an innocent bystander. Then Whittiker touched off the big gun again. It almost drove him out of the saddle but it scattered men right and left. As they swung onto the military road he turned around and sent the contents of the other barrel back toward Demerest but by this time the street was empty.

Tap and Whittiker pulled up about two miles out, letting their horses blow. "Figure they'll come after us?" Whittiker asked.

"Doubt it. By the time they get together enough saddled horses--and sober men to ride them--we'll be half way to the fort." Tap took the time to reload his revolver. "Anyway, Shipley's just a town marshall. We have as much right to shoot at him out here as he does at us."

"Fine! There's a thicket of willows 'bout four miles further on. Let's wait there. If they do come, bet I can clear two dozen saddles with both these barrels."

Tap shook his head. "Whit, you're a bloodthirsty old goat. Come on." He put Joshua into motion. "Let's get back to the fort. I want to catch the colonel before he gets his bed too warm."

It was a little after twelve midnight. Deacon Slater sat at the desk in Ben Shipley's office at the rear of the mercantile, drumming a pencil on a small pad of paper. Across the desk, sitting in a chair, was the marshall himself, fidgeting. There

84

were two other men in the room. One was Will Martin, sometimes deputy for Shipley. The other was Ab Miller, looking decidedly uncomfortable.

"You've done yourself proud, Marshall Shipley," Slater said. I leave town for a few hours and you manage to get several men shot up and put holes in half the business houses in town. Congratulations."

Shipley's fidgeting increased. "Wasn't my fault. It was that damned scout from the fort..."

"Was he causing a problem, Marshall?" Slater asked condescendingly, tilting his head to one side. "Was he disturbing the peace?"

The marshall was silent, sitting with his head hung down, staring at the floor. Then Slater shifted his attention to Ab. "What was going on in that bar, Mister Miller?"

Ab shrugged. "Nothing, Mister Slater. Man was just having a beer..." He looked at Ben Shipley who glanced up at the barkeep and gave him a cross look.

"And Marshall Shipley came in and declared that Scout Duncan was under arrest?"

"Didn't exactly say he was under arrest..." Ab licked his lips, glancing nervously at Shipley again. He didn't like being in a position where he had to put the marshall on the spot. "Just said that he was taking Tap...the scout, in."

Slater's eyebrows shot up slightly. "Do you know Scout Duncan, Mister Miller?"

"He's been in once before..."

"And you got to know him well enough to use his first name...?"

"Well..." Ab's discomfort was becoming more visible now. "Kind of knew him...by sight, anyway. From Wichita. He used to be a lawman there." Ab didn't like the way Slater's eyes bored into him. "It was some years back."

"All right, Mister Miller." Slater bowed his head toward the door. "Thank you for your help. You can leave...for now."

Ab didn't like the sound of that but he kept his mouth shut. He threw another glance at Shipley, who was looking back at him, his eyes hard. "Sure...anytime..." he mumbled. Ab left the little office and a few seconds later the front door of the mercantile rattled shut.

"Man rides two hours into town at nine o'clock just for a beer?" Shipley said, sourly. "I don't believe it. Duncan was up to something..."

"Perhaps," Slater said, "but Scout Duncan has been sent To Fort McPherson for a specific reason. To find out who's bringing in weapons to the tribes." Slater picked up the pencil and started drumming with it again. "It makes little sense to confirm his suspicions toward us by rash acts..."

There was the sound of a door opening--this time to the rear of the building--and a moment later a round face wearing a derby appeared in the doorway. "Mister Slater? Sorry to bother you..."

Slater stopped the drumming. "Quite all right, Griffin my boy. What is it?"

"Someone broke into the building in back. Tore the hasp right off."

For the first time, Slater's features took on some animation. "William? What do we have in there?"

Will scratched his head. "Wagon. Some gear. That's all."

"No guns? No packing crates?"

"No sir, Mister Slater. Just the wagon."

Slater leaned back in the chair, his face returning to its usual expressionless facade. "It would seem, Marshall Shipley, that I owe you an apology. Obviously, Scout Duncan was using himself as a decoy while someone broke into our property." He was quiet for a few moments, only a slight working of the muscles in his long jaw betraying that there was something going on behind his bushy eyebrows.

Slater came forward again, his elbows on the desk, his hands cupped around his chin. "I am especially outraged in that our own domain was invaded. This is a breach I cannot overlook."

Slater was quiet for a few moments, as if deep in thought. Then he turned to Will. "William. Go over to the Demerest House. There are two men staying there. John Eastland and Gabriel Yates. They're hiders heading out to the herd that passed through last week."

86

Then Slater stood, bending over the desk. "Tell them I have a little work here that will prove quite remunerative to them."

"What? Renumer...what?" Will looked confused.

"They can make a goodly sum of money," Slater said. "Tell them that."

Will pushed away from the wall and headed for the door. "And, William."

"Yes sir, Mister Slater?"

"In the morning, after you've eaten, go to the livery and check out one of our saddle stock. Young Griffin here will be making a ride to the fort."

13

It was a little after midnight and Colonel Bruster also sat at desk, this one in the headquarter's building of Fort McPherson. Instead of tapping with a pencil he twiddled with one of the tassels on the end of his robe tie. Tap had gotten him out of bed only fifteen minutes before and Bruster had taken him to his office, mainly to keep Matty from joining the discussion. His sleep-fogged brain was still sorting out what the scout had told him about Slater. Tap obmitted his run-in with Wolf Whistle and the possibility that Crazy Horse was in the area. He wanted to check that out a little further before creating a problem where there might not be one.

The room, the biggest office in the building, was about twelve by sixteen feet. The colonel's desk sat across the room from a large table, set with slat-backed chairs for staff meetings. On the wall above the table was a map of the United States. Below it hung a smaller one of the Department of the Dakota, in which Bruster's command lay. The only chair occupied at the table was the one that held Tap. He had pushed it back against the wall on two legs and, with his hands across his stomach and his hat pulled down over his eyes, was waiting for the colonel to speak.

"So," the colonel finally said, "You think Deacon Slater is behind the supplying of repeating rifles to the hostiles?"

"Yeah," Tap said from under the hat brim. "He's got the equipment. He's seems to have half the gun-toting citizens of the town on his payroll. I find him out on the grass right after I see new guns in Wolf Whistle's band... How the hell he's managed to keep from running across a patrol, I don't know."

Tap dropped the chair down and leaned across the table, his hands folded in front of him. "What you planning to do, Colonel?"

Bruster ran a hand across his face, brushing at the sleep-grit in his eyes and yawning. "For now, nothing."

"Nothing?" Tap sat upright.

"I'm afraid so. While I don't doubt anything you've told

me, if I were to arrest Slater, or have the federal marshall in Stanholp do so, I don't think anything you've told me would add up to a good case."

Tap looked exasperated. "I admit I haven't got a Brady portrait of Slater handing over a gun and accepting wampum beads but..."

"I'm afraid it's going to take something close to that." Bruster pushed himself back from the desk, opened a drawer and fished out two glasses and a whisky bottle. Tap walked over, took the glass the colonel proffered him, and sat back down.

"Slater has a lot more power than just what you see in Demerest." The colonel swirled the amber liquid around in the glass a few times and then sipped it. "He's a powerful man. Has interests territory-wide. He has strings that go right up into the territorial government--and beyond. If I make a premature move--one I can't back up--Slater needs only to make a small pull on those strings. The men in the territorial government then need only make even smaller pulls to Washington."

Bruster downed the glass and poured another. "They in turn would make yanks on the strings that reach to this fort. Next thing, I'm back in Washington, sifting papers at some tiny desk in a forgotten part of the war department, a colonel until I retire--or was retired out."

Bruster got up and walked to the maps. "I'm not a glory hound like Hawthorne but I would like to see that star on my shoulder one more time before I go." He traced a finger along the Missouri River on the smaller map. "And I think the way to get it is to stay here and do what I can to keep the peace between the Sioux and the whites coming into the territory."

Tap sighed and stood up, flushing the entire contents of his glass down in one draught. "In that case, Colonel, I'd like to requisition a spare cavalry mount and get permission to ride to Stanholp. If I'm going to get you some proof, I think I might find it there."

Stable Call had yet to sound when Tap walked into the stable area the next morning. His shoulder was about healed up and he was able to pull on his old over-the-knee boots. It was going to be a long, hard pull and he preferred his old war gear for a ride like this. He wasn't surprised to see Captain Hawthorne waiting while two horses were saddled for a morning ride--his and Matty's. Tap ignored him and went for his own two animals, brushing them out and saddling Joshua.

Tap mused that it was a wonder the captain was able to see to his duties, what with all the attention he was giving Matty. He gritted his teeth. The woman was really putting the pressure to him--but she was right. He would have to sort out his feelings for her and soon. Then he went to the holding pens and picked out a big rangy roan that looked like it had bottom.

He slapped a set of bags over the back of the McClellen. It only held an oilcloth-wrapped piece of cooked beef and a few biscuits along with a small container of water and some spare shells for the rifle. He didn't plan to need much on the trail for himself. After putting the Spencer in a scabbard he'd borrowed from Whittiker, he took up the lead ropes to the two unsaddled horses, mounted and started to turn away.

"Hold it there, Scout Duncan!" Tap wheeled Joshua back around. "Yes, Captain?"

"Two extra horses?" The captain stood with his hands on his hips. "You going into the business of breeding remounts?"

"These are all geldings, Captain," Tap said, making a sour face. "I'm riding to Stanholp. Expect to be back by evening. Figure," he tilted his head toward the two spare horses, "should be able to make it, changing off with these."

Hawthorne looked like he was going to say something more but before he could, Tap moved the horses out of the stable grounds and up to the headquarter's area. There he saw Sergeant Quinn standing on the porch, in front of the quartermaster's stores.

"Got yerself some spares?" Quinn called out. He smiled, making the white scar he had on his left cheek, presented to him by one of Stuart's men at Brandy Station twelve years before, stand out on his sun-reddened face.

"Heading for the railhead. Should be back for dinner, I push these nags along smart." He waved and kicked Joshua into motion across the parade ground and toward the fort entrance.

Tap put the big bay into an easy lope and for the next two

hours he changed off horses every half hour, never slacking the pace. Around ten o'clock he let the horses rest for thirty minutes while he wolfed down the biscuits and meat. Then he tightened the cinch and took off again, this time mounted on the cavalry horse. It was around noon when he rode into the railhead at Stanholp, the fifty-odd miles covered in five hours.

Tap left the horses at a livery with instructions to wipe, water, and cool them down. "Give 'em some grain, too," he added, "but go light on the hay. I'll be needing them for the ride back in an hour or so." Having his priorities, Tap stopped first at a saloon for a quick beer and then headed for the railroad station.

The station agent on duty was a stocky, balding man with a broken front tooth. It gave him a slight lisp. He glanced up at Tap from under a green eyeshade. "Sorry," the man said, rearranging a stack of papers on his desk. "Don't think I can let you see official railroad records..."

Tap tipped his hat back and leaned a hand on the agent's desk. "Look. I'm working for Colonel Bruster out of Fort McPherson. Trying to get a line on some illegal goods being sold to the Sioux." He put on his most sincere tone of voice. "Really need your help on this." He reached into his pocket and put a gold eagle on the man's desk. "Be glad to pay for your time..."

The man looked at the ten dollar gold piece, then up at Tap and back to the coin. "OK." He flipped the eyeshade up. "Just between you and me, eh?"

Tap nodded his head. "My lips are closed tighter than a tick on a hound."

Tap spent the next half hour going through waybills. He was only interested in the past few months and it didn't take long to find three different groups that looked like paydirt.

"These shipments," he said, spreading some waybills out in front of the agent. "Eight in three months for this outfit, the Dakota Territorial Supply. Three in the last two weeks for Geo. Kirby and Co. And six in the past two months, most of them eight to ten days apart, for the Northern Star Mine. What were they?"

The clerk looked over the waybills for a few moments then

brightened. "Well, the Territorial Supply is a lumber outfit. Wood. Sells finished lumber all over the territory--wherever they don't have trees or a mill. Pretty important account."

"You've seen the wood?"

"Oh my, yes," the agent said, lightly spraying the waybills through the gap in his teeth. "Big stacks of it. Takes up a whole flatcar."

"What about old Geo. here? What's Kirby about?"

"Booze. Supplies several saloons here and in other towns. Even more important than the wood."

"And this one?" Tap touched a third stack of waybills.

The agent adjusted his eyeshade. "Oh. Mining machinery. For the Northern Star Mine."

"Mining machinery? From a Saint Louis mercantile outlet?" Tap said, dubiously. "Where are they located?"

The man shrugged. "Beats me. They show up on the day the train brings the boxes in..."

"Do you know ahead of time when they're coming?"

No, but they do. They're always here to get the boxes."

"How many boxes?"

"Usually enough to fill the two wagons they bring."

Tap shuffled through the papers. "Who signs for this stuff?"

The clerk pointed to a signature scrawled along the bottom of a waybill. "Right there. A Mister Hawkins."

"What's this Hawkins look like?"

The man scratched his bald spot. "Oh, young. Ruddy complexion. Wears a derby hat, except once, when it was raining and he had on a sombrero...a wide brimmed hat."

"Any first name?"

The agent squinted up his face in thought. "Think I heard one of the teamsters call him 'Griff.'"

Tap felt a stab of elation. Apparently Slater let the little moon-faced gunman sign his waybills for him.

"Thanks for your time," Tap said. He turned toward the door, and then stopped. "Oh, one thing more. What were they using to haul these wagons?"

"Mules. Eight-up hitch."

Tap stopped for a last beer and a quick bite of food at

93

Chinaman Charlie's Chowhouse, an eatery near the stable. It was nearly two in the afternoon when he stepped back into the saddle, cinched down on Jericho, and leading the other two horses, headed out of Stanholp. Tap was satisfied in making such a hard ride. With one exception he learned about what he'd hoped to learn. Tap still didn't know when the next shipment would be along. Figuring from when the last one arrived, it had to be soon, maybe the next day or so.

Tap stopped to make his fourth change of horses on the return leg around four-thirty. This put him astride the cavalry mount. A few minutes later he crested a hill and pulled up, stopped by something he saw below. He'd been backtracking on his ride earlier that day, the path through the long grass quite visible. Now, down below, about a quarter mile away, he saw a new path leading off to his right, toward a jumbled rock outcropping. From the lower level this secondary path wouldn't be so noticeable but from his elevation it stood out. Whoever was waiting in those rocks was no Indian. An Indian wouldn't make a mistake like that.

So, Tap thought. He was being trailed and now set up for an ambush. He had no idea how many men might be in those rocks and he figured the simplest solution was to ride to his left, giving the outcropping a wide berth. His horse was fresh enough to outrun anything anyone in the rocks would likely have.

Tap slid out the Spencer, checked the chamber for a round, cocked the hammer, and held the carbine across the pommel. After trotting about three-hundred yards, he moved sharply left, finally putting about eight-hundred yards between himself and the rocks. Not enough, it turned out.

His horse broke wildly to the left, leaping up and shrieking in pain. Tap had just an instant to glance toward the rocks where he saw a puff of dirty white smoke. The clap of the shot didn't wash over him until he'd hit the ground, his head whipping into a rock some ten feet away from the thrashing animal. Tap wasn't unconscious but his head was full of cobwebs. He lifted a hand to his forehead and could feel the sticky warmth from a deep gash over his left eye.

Tap shook his head clear and swiveled around, trying to keep from moving any grass as he found the rifle. He checked the chamber again, found he'd triggered off a round as he fell, and levered in a fresh round. Then he brought the carbine to his shoulder, facing the rock outcropping. He slipped the barrel over the top of the now-still cavalry horse.

Tap wondered where Joshua and Jericho were but he couldn't take the time to look around for them now. Coming across the prairie were four horsemen, spread out, moving slow. In the hands of the one to his right was a long-barreled rifle and he could see the glint of sun off something above that barrel--a telescope! By God, he thought, it's a long-range buffalo gun!

Tap carefully eared back the hammer on the Spencer, taking a bead on the long-rifle bearer. Around two hundred yards out the four stopped, appearing to hold a confab with each other. It was long range for the lightly charged Spencer but he was afraid they might separate and come in from different directions--or perhaps on a run. Best to take a decent chance of a shot now than a poor one later. At the crack of the rifle the man with the buffalo gun threw his head up, then, slowly, tumbled off the back of the horse.

The other three riders were galvanized into action. The two who had been in the middle spurred their mounts forward, one loosing off a string of shots that surprised Tap by their rapidity. He sent a bullet off at the man, missed, and, disgusted with himself, steadied for the larger target--the horse. The man suddenly disappeared into the grass as the horse went down. Tap quickly shifted the sights of his rifle to the next closest rider...only he had turned off at seeing his companion drop and was now making dust toward the west and the direction of Demerest. Tap threw a couple of shots to speed him on his way, apparently without any effect, and then he turned back toward the other two men.

The man who'd gone down with his horse was nowhere in sight but the last mounted man had slipped off his horse and was standing, shielded by the animal, about a hundred yards away. He was aiming the rifle at Tap over the top of his saddle. The man fired, causing Tap to dive down beside the carcass, hearing--and feeling--the bullet slap into the body of the downed cavalry horse.

Tap peeked over the horse to see his rival trying to control his own mount who, apparently, didn't like having a rifle shot across his back. The horse finally broke free, taking to its heels and following the horse and rider who had bolted earlier. The man with the rifle, now exposed, fired off another shot at Tap and then flopped down in the grass.

Tap half stood, hoping to see if he could tell where the man was hidden. He couldn't but he crouched and watched the area where the man had dropped. After a few moments he saw the tops of a section of grass move and he put a round from the Spencer into the base of it. Tap dove for the ground as two quick shots came back at him...from the grass at least twenty feet away from where Tap had put his shot. That told him he couldn't necessarily trust the waving grass to give the man away--and also that the man was armed with a repeater.

The grass around Tap was pretty well flattened by now and he decided it wasn't enough cover. If his antagonist was hidden by the tall grass, he wanted to be, too. Tap raised himself and fired one quick shot from the Spencer into the area where the last shots were fired from. Then he scuttled away into the grass, leaving the rifle by the horse. He drew his revolver, heading to the left of where he thought the man might be. He tried not to move until the light prairie breeze gusted across the top of the meadow, causing the grass tops to wave about.

This was hard work, Tap thought. He moved along, trying to keep his gun ready, his head up, watching all around him and still making as little noise or movement in the grass as possible. The smell of the ground and the grass mingled with his sweat to gather around him in a pungent aura. He stopped and raised himself above the grass, his view through the vegetation at ground level being limited to only a few yards.

That action gained him a bullet. It whizzed close by his ear, driving him down. But he bounced up again, quickly. Tap anticipated that the man with the rifle, lieing on the ground as he was, would have to change position slightly to jack in another cartridge and might give himself away.

Tap tossed two quick shots his general direction, hoping that the man who went down with his horse was out of the picture. He did it more to get an idea of where the man was than in any real hopes of hitting him. It worked. Just before he ducked back down he saw the motion of the man's arm, working the lever on some kind of rifle about one hundred feet away. Tap rolled several yards to his left and waited, hunkered over, while the man sent a shot into his old position, followed by two more.

Tap stuck his head up again, pistol cocked, sure he knew where his man would be...but he wasn't! A shot from twenty feet off the man's previous position drove Tap down again. Damn! This guy was pretty good! He rolled quickly to one side, but to his right this time--just in case. Sure enough, several shots tore through the grass near where Tap would have been had he repeated his earlier pattern of movement. Tap moved once more, sweating even harder now, both from the exertion and from the pressure this little game of hide-and-seek was putting on him. He rolled again and two more shots moved the grass not four feet away. Apparently this man had plenty of ammunition and was willing to sweep the grass around him, hoping to get Tap or drive him out of cover. Tap, with only twelve extra rounds in a cartridge box on his belt, couldn't afford such a luxury.

Tap made another move and came up against something hard--a fair sized rock. He started to shove it aside and then had an idea. The rock was about half the size of his head and reasonably round. Tap moved the Colt to his left hand and hefted the rock in his right. He got to his feet and stood in a half crouch, looking toward where the last shots had come from. Then, swinging his arm around like he was bowling a game of pins, he sent the rock bouncing across the ground. He shifted the Colt, cocked, to his right hand.

It worked! A man jumped up about thirty feet out, rifle to his shoulder, expecting to see Tap running. Instead, he saw the rock bend the grasses down as it thudded along the ground. His mistake realized, he quickly turned toward Tap, swinging the rifle about. Too late. Tap's first shot caught the man full in the chest, driving the rifle out of his hands. The man made a stab for his pistol but Tap's second--and third--shot followed the first and the man was down. Tap reloaded his Colt and then walked over, cautiously. He picked up the man's Henry rifle--he could use this--and looked down into the face of someone he'd seen with Slater and the pack mules. He wouldn't be running any more guns to the tribes.

Tap noticed Jericho and Joshua feeding not far away and then looked toward the downed horse and rider. He saw movement and knew he still had a potential problem there. He circled the man and saw he was pinned under his horse. Tap ignored him for a moment but kept his distance. He walked over to the man with the telescope-equipped rifle. He didn't recognize him but he wasn't anyone's concern now but the buzzards. The man under the horse was a different matter. Held by one leg, he still was able to peer over the top of the animal, pistol in hand. Tap stood off a good one hundred feet or so and called to him.

"Toss the gun away, friend. I can pick you off real easy from here, I have a mind to." He held up the Henry.

"The hell with you!" the man said, sending a shot in Tap's direction. Tap lifted his rifle but then lowered it again. The man was now clicking an empty pistol. He walked toward the man, who, he had to admit, had guts. He kept the rifle ready just in case the man had a hideout. When he walked up, the man let the gun drop around one finger. Tap noted it was a Starr .44 self-cocker, which explained the rain of lead.

"I would'a beefed you," the man said., "but I dropped the caps. Only got one chamber reloaded." He held the Starr up, feebly, and Tap reached out and took it.

The man fell back, staring skyward, helpless--and Tap recognized him from the run-in with Shipley. It was the big man named Will. The horse, though dead, still carried a froth of lather. These men hadn't been waiting for him long.

"I only left for Stanholp a few hours back. How did you know to get out here so fast?" Will was silent and Tap hunkered down next to him, leaning on the Henry. "Tell me, friend. Who paid to set this up?"

"The hell with you!"

"Well, now," Tap said, standing. "Looks like you aren't in a real good position to chaw such a tough plug."

"Less'n you plan to kill me, someone'll come lookin' fer me, soon enough." The man's tone was resigned but defiant. Tap had to admire him.

"Lot's of Indians about..." Tap left the rest dangle.

"Ain't afraid of Injuns."

Tap thought on that a moment. "Could be they'd know you? Consider you a friend because of the guns you bring?"

"Go to hell!"

Tap put the rifle down and kneeled next to the man again, drawing a knife from his belt. As he did, he could see Will's head come up, his attention caught at last.

"Wha...what the hell you goin' to do?" he asked as Tap cut into the still-warm hide, starting to skin the horse.

"I lived with the Sioux a long time. Heard of a trick they liked to play on some enemy they didn't really care much for. Take a green buffalo hide, wrap 'em in it and leave 'em out in the hot sun." Tap glanced back at the man as he started to pull back some hide. "Skin shrinks down. Man dies. Real slow. Eyes bug out. Tongue hangs down a foot out'a your face. Never saw it done myself but this is as good a time to try as any. Horsehide ought to work almost as good as buff."

"You're crazy!" Will said, up on his elbows." "You ain't gonna..."

Tap swiveled around, the bloody knife in his hand, his eyes gimleted down. "Oh yes I am, friend! A while back I almost got burnt to death at a torture stake. I hold you and Slater part to fault on that. If it wasn't for the guns you run in, the Sioux wouldn't be so ready to fight. You don't tell me what I want to know, you'll be smellin' the insides of this hide for a couple days..." Tap looked at the hot sun, still a long way from setting. "Maybe not that many. Anyhow, I'll be back out in two-three days, just to see how it worked."

Will stared at Tap for a few seconds, didn't see anything there that made him think the scout was running a sandy on him, and then gave in. "OK," he said, resigned. "What do you want to know?"

"Slater running guns to the Sioux?"

"Yeah. Any other Injuns that want 'em, too."

"When's the next delivery?"

The man gave Tap a desperate look. "Honest! I don't know! Slater, he don't tell us that. Just has us hang around until he needs us. But soon, I'm guessing."

"How'd he know I was going to the railhead?"

"Don't know that, either." Will shrugged. "Your trail was easy enough to follow, but I don't know who told him."

Tap felt like the man wasn't giving him the whole story but he had enough. If he wanted to get back to McPherson before it was dark he had to end this now.

Tap stood, tossed the Starr a ways off, where he could find it later, and checked out the two bodies. In going through their pockets he turned up two-hundred and seventy dollars. The first man he'd killed was spread out over a long barreled Sharps rifle. His horse stood nearby, held there by a rein looped around the man's wrist. Tap retrieved the buffalo gun and went back to where Will was pinned and used the rifle to pry the horse up enough to get his leg out. Finding it broken, Tap splinted it with the rifle and strips of rawhide cut from the dead horse. Then he took the horse off the dead man's wrist and helped Will on board. It would be a long, painful ride into Stanholp for him...but it was better than lying out on the prairie.

"How much they pay that guy to kill me?"

Will avoided meeting Tap's eyes. "One hundred dollars. A piece. That was for the buffalo hunter and his friend...the one who made tracks. Fifty fer each of us." He nodded toward the man Tap had chased around in the grass.

Tap counted out one hundred dollars and put it in the man's hand. "Here. I'll keep the rest to pay for the government horse. That'll get your leg fixed in Stanholp and pay for your keep until you can get around again. After that, I'd suggest you dust out of this part of the country."

The man nodded. "Thanks. I will." His voice held a note of sincerity in it. "I mean it."

Tap pulled the saddlebags off the dead horse and tied them in back of the man's saddle. He patted them, found a little Colt .31 in it and shucked off the caps, handing the gun and handful of caps to the man. "Load 'er back up down the pike a ways." Then he slapped the horse and sent the man off toward Stanholp.

Tap gathered up all the firearms--and anything else useful he could find--retrieved the army saddle from the dead horse and packed up the plunder. He looked back on the two dead men. He didn't have a shovel to bury them with. He shrugged. What the hell, he thought. They wouldn't have bothered to bury him. That's what the buzzards were for. Then he set out for the fort.

It was dark when Tap rode into McPherson. He tied up at the doctors house and rattled the knob but the door was locked. Then Tap saw a shape sweeping toward him.

"Tap? Is that you Tap?" In a second Matty was in his arms. "I was so worried when you weren't back by dark." Her voice was small and tight. "Father said you should have been back by supper..."

"Had a little run-in with some fellas..."

She ran a hand over his forehead and felt the crusted blood. "You've been cut!"

"Scraped up is more like it..."

She turned and ran back toward her father's office. "Wait there!" she called out. A few moments later Matty returned with a key.

"Doctor Gates is in Demerest. A woman with a difficult birth..." She opened the door and pulled Tap in and then lit a lamp. She spent the next few minutes working on cleaning his wound, clucking away with the kinds of words women use in such circumstances--barely audible, seemingly breathless, mildly castigating. Her ministrations finished, she stood back, the light falling across her auburn hair.

Tap reached out and touched her hand. "All these years...you still look like a girl of seventeen..."

Body and spirit, Tap was weary from the ride and the fight. He realized that, right then, folding into Matty's softness was the most important thing on earth to him.

"I loved you when I was seventeen, Tap."

"Yes. And I you." He spoke his words more quietly than he could ever remember speaking. "And you still love me?"

"Yes, but perhaps a bit less strong."

He drew her to him. "Maybe," he said, the words slightly muffled by his face pressing against her breasts, "if I worked at it, I could make it strong again."

14

A half hour more passed before Matty and Tap took their leave of the doctors quarters, Matty locking the door behind her. There was no need to blow out the light as they had extinguished that long before...

Matty walked off to officer's row and her father's house and Tap started across the parade ground, toward the scout's quarters. Then he realized he had the infirmary keys and he turned toward the office buildings where he saw a light still shining in the colonel's office. Bruster would want to hear what he found out in Stanholp. He might as well fill the colonel in now.

Bruster sat at his desk, dressed in shirtsleeves and open vest. He stared at Tap, now seated against the wall across from him with a glass of whisky in his hand. "So! It is Slater!"

"Yep." Tap took a swig from the glass. "Could have hauled this Will guy back, broken leg and all, for you to listen to. But I figured the waybills, and whatever testimony you'd need from the freight agent..." Tap put down the now empty glass. "If you want more, I figure a raid on Slater's place at the right time..."

"No," Bruster said, standing. "I'm not too sure this gunrunning isn't a civil matter. I think I'll send a courier into Stanholp for the federal marshall and get his opinion."

Tap started to protest, "That could take time..." but the colonel put his hand up.

"I know, I know. We'll just have to increase our patrols and try to keep enough pressure on so that Slater won't be able to make deliveries."

Tap stood, disgusted but trying to keep it out of his voice. "Well, with the luck he's had at dodging patrols..." He let it go.

"You've had quite a trip" Bruster said. "You should get yourself a little sleep." The colonel poured another shot for himself as Tap opened the door to leave. "Tomorrow I may need all the scouts I have."

Tap detected something in the colonel's voice. "How's that?"

"Lieutenant Grimes went out on patrol earlier today. It was a short one and he should have returned by now. Probably no need for alarm. The Crow scout Kettle was with him. But if he hasn't returned by morning, I'll need to send you or Whittiker out with Captain Hawthorne to check on him."

"Hawthorne? Why him? He gets around Indians, it usually spells trouble."

"Because he's the only other officer I have who has some experience with fighting Indians. Grimes and Hawthorne are the only seasoned men I have assigned to me...well, there is Crossman. But he's been on detached duty to Washington for a few months. Sitting about with the other 'coffee coolers' I have no doubt." He reached out for the lamp and raised it to his lips. "That leaves me only Hawthorne to send out. Boots and saddles will sound at four A.M."

Tap left the colonel's office, biting his tongue to keep him from pointing out that Hawthorne's 'experience' consisted of attacking a peaceful camps and groups of women and children. Then he took Bruster's advice and rolled into his bunk as soon as he could. Not even Whittiker's snoring kept him from dropping right off to sleep.

The sun was just topping the distant hills when company 'C' left the fort. Whittiker and Tap ranged out ahead of the column, to either side, watching for a trail. During the night a cavalry horse had come in, blood on its saddle. Colonel Bruster decided the situation was serious enough to send out both scouts, and the Arikara scout, Broken Hand, to accompany Captain Hawthorne and a large force of troopers. After about an hour's ride to the north-east the two scouts, still roving ahead of the column, found the patrol's tracks...and then some.

"Looks like unshod horses followin' shod, " Whittiker said, on his hands and knees, looking down into the grass. "Best we wait until Hawthorne catches up. No tellin' what's ahead. Bunch of carbines might be nice to have about."

Ten minutes later the company, led by the 'Ree scout, caught up with the two men. "Grimes' men went through here, Captain," Whittiker said, pointing out the hoof marks in the hard packed ground. "Looks like he was bein' trailed by Injuns."

The scout, still dismounted, turned and tightened his cinch. "A fair number, too."

"Then for God's sake, let's go!" Hawthrone shouted, moving ahead of the scouts and spurring his horse--and the column of troopers, riding in twos--past them both.

Whittiker and Tap exchanged glances. "Man in that big a hurry to find trouble," Whittiker said, "Got a good chance a finding it."

Hurriedly, he finished with his saddle and mounted. Both put heels to their mounts since they had fallen behind the column. They caught sight of it again within a few minutes, as it rode down into a shallow canyon.

The ground all along here was mostly broken into gentle, rolling hills but parts were heavily covered with brush and rocky outcroppings. The fastest way to move a horse across it was by keeping to established game trails. Grimes had apparently done just that--as was Hawthorne. Both men followed a natural trail down through a narrow cut rather than seek a longer but safer way around that would keep them to higher--and more visible-- ground.

Tap and Whittiker saw the column just as the last of it dipped down into the cut. They were several hundred yards back and at that distance could see what the soldiers could not-- Indians, hidden in the rocks above the cut. The warriors had stayed out of sight until the cavalrymen passed by, not expecting the scouts to be bringing up the rear. Now they were moving forward to fire down on the troopers.

Tap quickly fired his rifle--the Henry he'd taken from the dead man the day before--and shouted. The lieutenant leading the last section of troopers turned and saw the Indians taking up firing positions. He drew his sword and pulled his horse around, leading his men in a charge up and out of the cut.

The Indians started to fire down at Hawthorne and the rest of the troopers. Hawthorne, deciding a dash out would be suicidal, as far in as he was, dismounted and had his men take positions behind the boulders that lined the bottom and sides of the cut.

"Lieutenant Rogers!" Tap shouted as the officer pulled his small command up in front of the two scouts. "It's a trap..."

"I know, Mister Duncan. Thank you for your warning!" His horse, agitated by the action, danced around. "I think my best move is to charge those Indians on the left. Try to drive them off." He looked back at the Indians lining the rocks above the cut. There were more of them on the left side, the right having fewer rocks to hide behind.

"Yessir." Tap said. "But you'll never be able to take your horses in among them boulders."

"Right!" The lieutenant turned. "Sergeant Prinze! Dismount the men. Every fourth man a horseholder. The rest to charge on foot with me."

The officer swung down out of his saddle and turned the leathers over to a trooper. The big German sergeant started barking guttural orders--"Come on, poyz! Ve lick em! Dun't forget der extra bullets in der bags!"--while Whittiker and Tap quickly turned their own mounts over to a trooper, first taking several boxes of spare cartridges from their saddlebags.

"Lieutenant!" Tap yelled, as he moved off with his men. "Whit and I will try to keep the Indians on the right off your back!" The man waved his hand in assent and Tap and Whittiker moved down to a small outcropping of rocks just at the entrance to the cut. From here they had a good command of the right side of the shallow gorge. With their repeaters--they could make it hot for the few warriors who were using that side to fire down on Hawthorne and his men.

The two scouts started shooting at the Indians on the right. There weren't many targets but they kept heads down and, thanks to the boulders, sent ricochets bouncing around. "We don't run low of forty-four flats," Tap said, "This should keep them out of Hawthorne's hair."

Rogers and his men were fighting rock to rock, driving back the Sioux, who, with the element of surprise gone, weren't really interested in fighting on the soldier's terms. The pressure on him relieved somewhat, Hawthorne and several of his men managed to move close to the entrance of the cut, using the rocks as cover between dashes across open ground. This was brought to Tap's attention when, as he concentrated on the upper rim of the cut, a bullet hit the rock just to his rear and screamed off into the ether.

Tap looked up, startled. That shot had come from down below and he shifted his eyes to the cut where he saw Captain Hawthorne. The man was slapping the breech of his carbine shut, having just finished reloading. Then he lifted it to his shoulder and took aim in Tap's direction.

There was a second shot, this one going high, and Tap yelled, swinging his Henry around to bear on Hawthorne. "Dammit!" he shouted. "Are you crazy?" But Hawthorne just made a pointing gesture with his hand and then waved him off, turning away and giving his attention to the few Indians still engaging Rogers.

Mystified, Tap turned and looked behind the boulder to his rear. At its base, on one side, was an Indian, laid out on his back with a neat, round hole in his forehead. Near one outstretched hand was a war club. Tap looked closely at the man. It was the same one he'd seen coming out of the tipi in Wolf Whistle's camp...and once, behind the stables at Fort McPherson.

It didn't take long to secure the cut and the area around it. Indians largely fought as individuals and when confronted by a cohesive force of sufficient strength, they preferred to break off the fight until conditions were more favorable...or there was a greater reason to fight. A few of the soldiers were wounded and a horse or two lost but none of the whites had been killed. The Indians managed to pull off all their casualties.

Tap tried to thank Hawthorne for saving his life but he brushed him off. "I was killing Indians. Not trying to do you any favors," he said, testily. "If it's safe to move about, let's see if we can't find Lieutenant Grimes and his command." He mounted his horse. "That," his voice was cold, "is what we came out to do, I believe."

Whittiker, standing nearby, said to Tap, "If Grimes blundered into this cut like the captain did, I don't feel too prosperous about what we'll find."

Tap and Whittiker took the point, quickly picking up the trail. It didn't go far. It led about a half mile on to a grassy swale. There was brush lining the ground on the left side of the trail and, a hundred yards across, on the right, a small grove of trees. It was between these two points that the patrol was hit.

The eleven men and one Crow scout fell almost in line, taken by such surprise that there was little time to maneuver for defense. All the bodies were stripped and most were mutilated, some beyond recognition. Hawthorne, after one pass down the line of men, lying white as alabaster in the mid-morning sun, wheeled his horse around in front of Tap and Whittiker, his face contorted, his eyes ablaze.

"See?" he spit out, the saliva almost foaming at his mouth. "This is the kind of work you can expect from savages! Sheridan was right! They should all be killed off, to the last woman and child!"

"Was that what you had in mind when you hit that hide-stretching party?" Tap shot back, matching Hawthorne's anger. "That's probably what led to what you see here! At least these men were armed and looking for trouble!"

"God damn you!" Hawthorne yelled "You can't compare these men to heathen savages!" He whirled his horse about and dug in his spurs, driving the horse over to Lieutenant Rogers, standing his horse off to one side and trying not to look at a soldier who had been dismembered.

Tap and Whittiker moved their mounts away, down to what had been the head of the patrol. It was strange to look on the trooper's bodies. They were stark white compared to their owner's faces, reddened by months or years in the sun, so dark now in contrast as to make them appear almost like black men.

At the head of the little column four men were grouped about three horses. Perhaps here there had been a 'last stand.' One man was an Indian, undoubtedly the Crow scout named Kettle.

"Surprised he wasn't more careful," Whittiker said, looking down at the man whose body, since he was of the hated Crow tribe, had taken an extra measure of abuse from the Sioux. "Must'a been wool-gatherin' an not figurin' fer any hostiles this close to the fort."

Another body, the face too mutilated by a war axe to tell, was likely Lieutenant Grimes. He was a tall lanky man as was the corpse. Several dead Indian ponies were strewn about, which made both scouts agree that here at least a fight had been made.

Tap noticed something sticking out from under one of the dead horses and he dismounted to look it over. It was the stock of a rifle--he recognized it as a Spencer--broke off at the wrist when the animal had fallen. It contained a line of tacks around the outer part of the stock flat with a brass-tack cross in the center. Buffalo Lance!

Tap looked at Whittiker who seemed to recognize the pattern, too. "Guess that explains why they worked the dead over so good," the old scout said. "Evenin' up fer that raid Hawthorne made."

Tap put the stock in his saddle bag and was just mounting when Hawthorne rode up, slowly, his manner grim rather than explosive as a few minutes before.

"Scout Whittiker. I want you to take five men and return to McPherson. Have them come back out with wagons. To haul the dead. Have them bring tarpaulins, too." He wiped a hand over his eyes. "We don't need to have the women see what we bring in."

"Whittiker nodded and moved off toward five troopers standing their mounts near Lieutenant Rogers who, even from a hundred feet away, was obviously still green about the gills. Tap and Hawthorne clucked their mounts into motion, riding together, silently, back along the sad line in front of them.

"All right! Killing! But why the mutilation? The ghoulishness? There's no reason for it!" The captain's voice was heavy with disdain.

"Their way of life is different than ours, Captain," Tap said, doubtful the man would understand but willing to try. "They don't see things same as us. Put out a man's eyes, even if he's dead, he can't see to get to heaven. Has to roam around the spirit world, blind."

"See that!" Tap pointed to a rock with two pieces of something that looked like bloody dried peaches on it. "Ears. Their way of saying, 'Can you hear us now? Will you listen to our cries to be left alone? To keep our land?' Something like that. That's what they were trying to say by putting those ears there."

Hawthorne just shook his head, feeling numb from sights he

never before had to endure, even on the cannon-torn killing fields of the war. "They're not like us," he said, finally. "We can never live with them and we aren't likely to change them." He straightened in the saddle. "We can only kill them off or drive them into reservations, where we can hold them for a few centuries, until their culture breeds out of them."

Hawthorne swiveled his head to settle eyes filled with hate on Tap. "As for yourself! A squaw man I've heard! Not one whit better than they!" Hawthorne spit his words out in precise bits. "Yet," he said, with as much contempt as he could muster, "you aspire to the hand of a colonel's daughter!" He yanked his horse about and moved toward a knot of cavalrymen placing blankets over the remains, leaving Tap to his own dark thoughts.

15

Tap had been ordered to lead the column to the patrol. He'd done that. As far as he was concerned, he could now go back to the other assignment given him by Bruster--searching for the gunrunners. He tightened his cinch and, over the protest of the captain, took his leave. The column was big enough to take care of itself, if Hawthorne didn't do something stupid--a distinct possibility, Tap mused dryly. And he had a good 'Ree scout, Broken Hand, to watch over him--if he'd listen to an Indian.

However, Tap wasn't going looking for gunrunners, not just yet, anyway. The thing that needed to be done was to make sure that the guns already in the hands of the warriors weren't used in a territory-wide Indian war...and after what happened to Grimes and his men, that would take some doing. Tap knew if there was any chance of avoiding a conflict it would depend on two men; Colonel Bruster and Wolf Whistle.

When he'd been in Wolf Whistle's camp, the chief had mentioned the grass there was wearing thin and the band was preparing to move. Tap's last swing through this country had been in eighteen sixty-seven. He'd been on a horse stealing raid against the Crow with some warriors from Two Knives' band of Cheyenne. As he recalled, there was a lush, grassy area near the Heart River where there was good feed for the horses and the women could gather berries and edible roots. The place on the Heart would be a logical camp ground for Wolf Whistle's band to go, Tap thought, and he turned Joshua south-east, toward the river.

Almost three hours later Tap rode down into the Indian camp and dismounted. Wolf Whistle walked up to greet him along with Horse Catcher. "Ho, brother! We are glad you came. Our stores are fat and we will roast a buffalo haunch in your honor!"

"Better than the time," Tap said with a grin, "when you wanted to roast me." He took the hand of both men. Wolf Whistle looked embarrassed at being reminded of the incident but Tap laughed and Horse Catcher joined in.

"Don't worry, my brother," Horse Catcher said to Wolf

Whistle. "He will have a good story to tell over the fire at night to his grandchildren, about how Buffalo Lance almost killed him."

Tap's face turned serious. "Where is Buffalo Lance?"

"Gone," said Horse Catcher. "The other day, after our council meeting. He said the whites really don't want peace. Most of the men from the Sacred Arrow Bundle Society left with him. Only a few stayed. Some who have families." The chief looked downcast. "I'm afraid he is going to make council with Crazy Horse again. And then war will come."

"Listen to my words, Wolf Whistle. War has already come." Some tribal wise men and military leaders had gathered around the three and Tap directed his words to the circle of men.

"Today, this morning, the soldiers had a fight with warriors, north of here. We found ten soldiers who had been killed the day before."

Alarm showed in Wolf Whistle's face. "Crazy Horse and his warriors...maybe it was they..."

Tap lifted the flap to his saddlebag and reached into it. "I found this on the war ground, where the dead soldiers were," he said, handing the tack-studded piece of wood to Wolf Whistle.

Wolf Whistle took the broken Spencer stock and turned it over in his hands. "Yes," he said sadly. "This belonged to Buffalo Lance. Now there will be war."

"Maybe not," Tap tried to make his voice sound encouraging. "We may be able to keep the peace if you'll talk with the white chief of the fort. Are you willing to try?"

Wolf Whistle looked at Tap with dark, sad eyes. "Will it do any good?" he asked.

"It's worth a try, to keep your people and mine from dying. Where can we meet?"

"An hour from here, there is a place called Old Buffalo Meadow. Snow-On-His-Face knows the spot," Wolf Whistle said, referring to Whittiker. "We can meet there tomorrow, when the sun is just starting its slide to the edge of the earth." The chief swept his arm across the breadth of his camp. "I will come alone. Only my war chiefs and wise men will be there." His jaw took on a firmness. "If the white chief has a good heart, have

112

him come with only as many as fingers on one hand."

"I don't know how many he'll bring," Tap replied, "but he won't be coming with the whole fort. I'll see to that."

Tap grasped the arms of both Wolf Whistle and Horse Catcher and then mounted his horse. "If I can't get the white chief to come, I'll be there anyway. But," he swung his horse about, "I think he'll come."

Tap headed back toward the fort. The sun, in an almost cloudless sky, brought considerable heat to the day and the cavalry mount he rode had a sheen of sweat on him. He'd have preferred to ride one of his own horses but, after yesterday, he felt they deserved a rest. Tap had ridden about three hours when, while he crossed a stretch of dry rocky ground, he noticed a moving figure, off to his right, coming at an angle that would intersect him. He could see it was a white man and, in another few minutes, made him out to be Whittiker.

"Hey, old son. A ways from the Captain, ain't ya?"

"You too," Tap retorted. "What you doing out here?"

"Soldiers don't need me to drive ambulances. Thought I'd look around fer them wagon tracks you told me about. Found these." He pointed down. "Wagons. Two of 'em."

Tap circled the area Whittiker indicated and, after a few turns, made out the faint scratches in the hard ground. "Fresh! Maybe a day old, at most!"

"More like hours," the old scout said, tersely. "Surprised the dust had time to settle."

Tap looked at Whittiker. "Then they damn near beat me out of Stanholp yesterday!" He pulled his hat off and ran a hand through his hair. "Slater must have had a shipment due in later that day or evening. But why did they swing so far south? It almost looks like they knew that patrol was out there."

"Dunno. Tracks look like they head for Demerest, though. Think we ought'a tell Bruster?"

"No." Tap said. "They could have them on mules and out of there before we got to McPherson." Tap thought for a moment while Whittiker sucked on the end of a stalk he pulled from a lone clump of tall grass nearby. He needed to see the colonel--to get a meeting with Wolf Whistle set up. At the same time, keeping another load of repeaters out of the hands of the hostiles was important too. Tap made a decision.

"Slater knows I'm still alive," Tap said. "He's going to get any guns he has out of Demerest, just in case the army comes snooping around. Get them out to Buffalo Lance, Crazy Horse or whoever. Think we might see if we can't put the quietus on that."

Tap swung his horse around, and lined him out toward Demerest. "Follow me," he yelled at Whittiker, who, startled by Tap's actions, spit out the reed and put his own horse into motion. "Wolf Whistle said you know where Old Buffalo Meadow is," Tap said as Whittiker caught up. "You tell me where and I'll tell you why I need to know."

It was dusk when the two men crested the hills above Demerest. The stars were beginning to wink on in the descending blackness and oil lamps in the town below matched them. They moved at a walk through the brush until it gave way to a rough, rutted track. This soon became a side street leading to Demerest's main road, passing right by the corner where sat the Dakota Queen. Tap held up when they reached the back street that ran down the rear of the saloon, parallel to the main road. There was a figure outside, sitting in a highbacked chair, smoking a cigarette. It looked a little like Miller and Tap, thinking Ab might be taking a break, called out to him.

"Ab! That you?"

The man tilted his head back, looking at the two horsemen. In the lowering gloom he wasn't able to recognize who was calling. "Who's that?" he asked.

"Friend of Ab's," Tap said back, realizing this wasn't Miller. "Ab around?"

"Naw. Ain't been in for two days. Was thinkin' a checking up on him after shift tonight." The man stood, flipped the cigarette butt away and reached for the back door. "You wanna look in on 'em, his place is that one there." He pointed back up the cross street. "Third on the left."

Whittiker scratched his chin. "Why you lookin' fer Miller?"

"Thought he might be able to tell us what's been going on in town," Tap said, but his voice held a concern that had nothing to

114

do with his desire for information. "I don't like the sound of this--Ab not being seen for two days. Let's check out his place."

Tap and Whittiker rode the couple hundred feet to Ab's house--really a rough lean-to, little more than a shed. Tap dismounted and handed the reins to Whittiker. "Be out in a minute, Whit. Any trouble, whistle."

Tap knocked and, not hearing anything, pushed on the door. It made a scraping sound as the bottom dragged across the uneven floor. "Ab?" Tap called, softly. "Ab?"

He heard a noise--more like the sound of a hurt animal--and he pulled out a match and struck it. "Ab?" he said, again. Tap moved toward the dim outline of a man laying on a cotton mattress supported by a rough wood bedstead. "What the...?"

Tap spotted a lamp on a small table, lit it, and walked to the bed, bending down. Ab Miller was stretched out on the mattress, clothed only in his longjohns, a tattered blanket pulled half-way up his body. His head was partly covered by a bandage and Tap could see the cuts and bruises on his face. Ab coughed--a harsh, racking cough that jarred his body--and then turned toward Tap.

"Who...?"

"Tap. Tap Duncan. What happened..?"

"Tap! You gotta get out of town..." Ab brought his hand up to his mouth as he coughed again and Tap reached out to steady the man's body.

"Never mind me." Tap said, feeling the anger rise within him. He had a pretty good idea of how Miller came to look like this but he wanted particulars. "What happened to you? Who did this...?"

"Slater. Had me worked over good. That next afternoon, after the rookus at the saloon." Ab's voice was weak and he wheezed out the words rather than spoke them. "Called me into the Marshall's office. Said I was a friend of yours. Wanted to know what you were about. Then he stood there and watched as that little bastard in the derby hat--Griff--pistol-whipped me." Ab coughed again and then had to wait a moment before he could go on.

"Griff said he'd just ridden in from the fort. That now they were going to hang you out to dry." Ab grimaced and propped

115

himself up on one elbow. "Got the impression they had someone in mind to do the job." Ab stopped to rest for a few seconds. Talking took more energy then he had to spare. "Then they all took turns working me over. Except Slater. He just watched...and grinned.

Ab put out a hand, clutching Tap's arm. "Didn't tell them nothin,' Tap. Not a damn thing. But you best take care." Ab flopped back down in the bed. "I think they're gonna send someone out to try and bushwhack you."

"Don't worry. Someone already tried. Now they're feeding the wolves." Tap touched Ab's bandaged head. "What about you? How bad you hurt?"

"Beat up. Kicked around. Got a couple broken ribs." Tap could see the weak grin in the dim light of the lamp. "Been beat up worse...but I was a lot younger, them days."

"You need a doctor..." Tap started to get up but Ab stopped him with a hand on his arm.

"Saw one. Sawbones from the fort was in town, sittin' in at some bargirl's babyin.' One a the girl's knew about this," Ab moved a hand down his body, "brought him by. I'll be OK. Worse part, Slater fired me. Said no saloon a his in town would hire me."

Tap stood, the tightness in his voice betraying the rising fury inside him. "Anything I can get for you, Ab?"

The man chuckled lightly--and even that hurt. "New head. This one sounds like muskets is goin' off in it."

"Keep your ears open," Tap said, grimly. "You may hear some more soon." He blew out the lamp and moved to the door and then stopped and looked back at Ab.

"About the job. Check back tomorrow, Ab...or as soon as you're able. The 'Queen just might be under new management."

Tap walked out and took the reins from Whittiker. "What took you so long?" the old man said, a bit agitated. "Everythin' OK?"

"Not for Ab."

"What's wrong?"

"Worked over proper."

"Slater?"

116

"And company." Tap's words were coming sparse and slow.

"I seen you like this before," Whittiker said, even in the dark sensing a change in the younger man's demeanor. "You plannin' on makin' this thing personal? 'Member, we ain't lawmen."

Tap pulled his Colt, breaking open the gate and slipping a cartridge into the chamber he usually kept empty and under the hammer. He set the hammer down between the heads of two shells and then returned the gun. "I've got me Judge Colt here and six provisions of his statutes," he said, coldly. "Think I'll go down and serve them up."

"Well, best you don't go direct. Looky down street."

It was completely dark now and Tap looked to the end of the back street, by the barn, two short blocks away. He could see lamplight spilling from the open doors of the structure. It cast a pool of brightness out onto the street in front and fell partly on a wagon parked hard up against the mule pen.

"I didn't have any warnin' we was to be socializin' so I didn't bring ol' Percy. Best we don't go in with no trumpet fanfares."

"OK. We Injun up on them from behind. Let's go."

Tap turned his horse back up the street they had come in on, past Ab Miller's and into the brush and grass that grew on the slight rise of ground behind the town. Then the two men cut to the right, riding across the hillside until they were opposite the barn and a few hundred yards above it, looking down.

They tied their horses in some brush and crept toward the mule pen, both holding their rifles at the ready.

The corral was full of mules and in the illuminated barn, fifty feet away, they could see a second wagon. Several men were milling about, carrying pack saddles.

"What you plannin' to do?" Whittiker said, his voice low. "Ask fer a peek in them wagons?"

Both men were behind the corral and just above the outside wagon. The mules started to move about, catching the strange scent and becoming uneasy over their approach. "Dunno," Tap said, whispering. "Just want to make sure those guns, if that's what they are, don't leave town."

A mule bolted, causing several others to panic and crash against the side of the corral. The outside wagon, jammed against the rails of the pen, rocked sideways and a crate slid off the back, over the tailgate. It landed near the rear of the wagon, one end shattered, and in the lamplight, Tap could see the barrels of several rifles protruding from the boxes' end.

"Hey!" someone shouted. "Who's out there?" and Tap saw men coming out of the barn. He stepped away from the side of the corral, around to the back of the wagon. He stood by the vehicle's gate, while Whittiker moved to Tap's left, into the shadows. Tap realized it was a bad spot, the light from the barn hitting him, but it was just as bad for the men by the barn doors, outlined against the same light.

"Drop your guns!" Tap yelled, and a figure that had looked to be standing with a shovel in his hands suddenly brought the 'shovel' up and unloaded one side of a shotgun at him. It missed but it made Tap drop his rifle. He threw himself to the ground, landing behind the smashed box of rifles as the second load tore into it, showering him with splinters. Tap swiveled around, his Colt out now, and peered over the top of the box. He drove a quick shot at the man--too quick, it missed--as the man clacked the gun closed on two new shells and raised the gun again. The trigger was never pulled. A burst of three shots from the darkness-- Whittiker--quickly settled his hash.

Tap was up now, crouching beside the mule pen. "Drop them!" he shouted again and another figure, one wearing the outline of a derby hat, his gun already out, answered with a shot that missed Tap and went into a penned mule. The resultant uproar from the wounded animal caused the others to thrash against the corral and Tap stumbled away from the boards, not certain they would hold the bolting mules. His heart was racing now and he knew he was exposed. He moved to his left, snapping off a shot at Griff and getting another back in reply. A shot came his way from a man by the door and then there was a roar from Whittiker's Winchester that caused the man to wilt, like a stem-cut flower.

Tap stayed focused on Griff and fired again. He saw the man reel sideways, then spin back around, only grazed. His mind racing, Tap continued to cat-walk left, hoping he wasn't moving into Whittiker's line of fire. He rested the Colt over his arm and fired once more and Griff's Smith .44 tilted, firing almost straight up as the gunman's knees buckled and he fell face forward.

Two other men still stood in the wide doorway. One suddenly took off on a run, back into the barn. He turned once, to snap a shot off over his shoulder with a pistol. Then Whittiker's rifle sounded and the man fell. "Always did like a movin' target," Whittiker cackled out of the darkness.

The other man slowly raised his hands. "I ain't armed," he said, his voice trembling. Tap walked over, warily, confirmed that the man was dehorned and then pushed him aside. Griff was dead and so was the man who had wielded the shotgun. The man by the door had been hit in the arm while, miraculously, the one who had turned to run was only unconscious. Instead of being shot, he'd stumbled, fallen and hit his head. Whittiker slapped a rag around the hole in the wounded man's arm, grousing about getting old and missing such an easy shot, while Tap noted one thing--nowhere in this pile of bodies could he find Slater...or Shipley.

Tap reloaded his Colt and moved cautiously out of a side door in the barn and toward the back of the mercantile. The door to the store interior was ajar. Tap stood to one side and pushed it open. He started to step in and then stopped. He had a better idea, and he turned and went back to the barn. "Whit! Get your rifle and keep an eye on the back door of the mercantile. I'm going in the front. Slater has got to be somewhere."

Tap ran around to the entrance of the mercantile, just in time to see the front door start to open. By the light of a single street lamp in front of the building, he could make out the gaunt, cadaverous form of Deacon Slater stepping over the sill. In his hand he held a big pistol that Tap recognized as a ten-shot LeMat.

"Hold it!" Tap yelled, and he started the Colt up to cover the man. Slater, for all his height, was not clumsy and, cat-like, he disappeared back into the dark of the store.

Tap hefted himself up onto the store platform and ran for the door just as Slater sent several shots through it. His momentum unchecked, Tap changed direction slightly and crashed through the big plate glass window, rolling to a stop against a pickle barrel in the center section. He looked down the left aisle and saw, by the light coming out of the doorway to Shipley's office, Slater just opening the rear door. Then a series of shots rattled out of the night and drove Slater back. Whittiker!

Tap was momentarily distracted by the big sections of glass he'd brought with him in his hasty entrance and he kicked some of it away, not wanting to become impaled on a large shard. He turned at a heavy clap of noise and a sudden darkness from the office and then realized Slater had put the lamp out of commission by using the center shot-firing barrel of the LeMat.

That meant it was now Tap who would be outlined by light--the streetlamp--if he showed his head around the other side of the aisle. Still, he tried. On his knees, Tap looked around the end of the center section and down the left-hand aisle. He drew a shot from Slater for his efforts and ducked back. His mouth felt dry. Facing a man straight on was one thing but he didn't like this cat-and-mouse game--especially when he felt like the mouse.

"Scout Duncan!"

"Yeah!" Tap shouted. "What?"

"We should not be adversaries. I'm a very powerful man in this territory. Freight offices in all the big settlements. Dealings with the railroads..." Slater's voice was low, calm and conciliatory. It made Tap think of a rattlesnake just before it strikes.

"Don't think I'd be interested in throwing in with a gunrunner. Or man who beats up good barkeeps. No thanks!"

"You're not looking at the business side of this, my boy..." Tap noticed that Slater's voice was changing volume. He must be moving down aisle, closer to where Tap sprawled, at the end of the center section and between the two aisles. Tap hefted the Colt, figuring that, in another moment or two, he could twist around the corner and get a good clear shot at the man, dark or no. Then he heard a rumbling noise overhead that didn't make sense. Tap's eyes were pulled toward the ceiling and in the

120

meager light that trickled in from the oil streetlamp outside, he saw something that made his heart jump in his chest. A barrel was rolling past the end of the overhead platform. Slater had been moving toward the lever that opened the gate!

Tap threw himself forward, into the left-hand aisle and next to the counter, just as the barrel crashed to the floor where he'd been. He twisted around as, twenty feet away, Slater aimed his pistol, hoping to get a bead on Tap in the near-dark of the store. A second barrel rumbled into place at the lip of the platform and Slater fired.

Slater missed and Tap shoved himself forward again, against the counter, trying desperately to avoid the second falling barrel that, when it hit the first, tumbled toward him. Tap loosed off two quick shots down-aisle but they went wild and he beat another retreat as a third barrel fell, splitting and sending beer cascading everywhere.

Tap started to get up but slipped in the beer, falling against the base of the counter...and then he heard another loud, rolling noise, this time at floor level. He began to rise again when he saw--dimly--the shape of something coming down the aisle at him. It took a second for him to realize it was a wheelbarrow, swiftly trundled along by Slater who was whooping wildly. Tap thumbed off a couple of shots but his low angle and the heavy wheelbarrow kept Slater covered. Slater stopped and dug in the prow of the wheelbarrow, uprighting it onto Tap. He then stood back and pumped four bullets through the bottom of the wooden wheelbarrow. He was just earing back the hammer to let off the last shot in his revolver when the door at the rear banged open and Whittiker levered off three quick rounds of .44 Henry flats.

Slater dropped his pistol and slowly turned around, his face frozen in a look of disbelief. Then, as if it took time for all that length of body to fold itself up, he fell against a support that held the overhead rack and crumpled to the floor. Whittiker walked down to Slater and used a toe to roll him over. Satisfied with what he saw, he turned and lifted the wheelbarrow off Tap.

"Am I dead? I've got to be dead. I feel heavy all over."

Whittiker reached down and pulled on the fifty pound sack of flour that pinned Tap. "Open yer eyes, old son. The flour sack took all the lead." He looked down at Slater. "Guess that's why you didn't get him either."

Tap got to his feet, brushing off the flour that, thanks to the beer, was sticking to him everywhere. "You got Slater?"

"Yep! Guess I ain't losing my touch, after all."

"Sure as hell missed him when he tried to go out the back!

"Didn't miss! Whittiker said, the hurt look on his face apparent even in the dim light from the street. "Was just drivin' him back inside. Thought you wanted to finish him personal."

Tap was exasperated. "You old goat! You could've got me killed!"

"Could not! Ya' had a wheelbarrow full of flour to protect you!"

Tap shook his head in disgust. "You don't know anything about wheelbarrows--or women!"

"Do too! One's good fer savin' yer back and doin' all the heavy work around the lodge. "T'other'll get all weather-cracked and creaky, ya' don't take care of it." He cackled. "Never 'member which is which, though."

"Go get the horses!" Tap said, wearily, unraveling a bolt of cloth to wipe some of the mess from himself.

When Tap returned to the barn there were several townsmen standing around. A few had started to look after the wounded while others were gathering up a few mules that had gotten loose. Then he heard a familiar--if not welcome--voice.

"What's going on here?" said Ben Shipley, walking up with his Greener in hand.

"What kept you, Marshall," Tap said. "You're usually right there when trouble starts...if you aren't the one who starts it."

"Ask one a the gals at the 'Queen where he was," an onlooker volunteered and several others laughed. Shipley flushed and glowered at the crowd, then brought the shotgun up.

"Maybe you want to answer some questions for Mister Slater..."

"Might be a wee bit careful a that, friend," Whittiker said, coming out of the shadows to tuck the barrel of his Winchester under Shipley's chin. "Slater's dead and you might just be the next feller on the list."

The marshall grinned weakly and lowered the shotgun.

"Slater and his men were running guns to the Indians, Marshall," Tap said. "Seems strange how you didn't know about that in a town this size." His voice held more than a hint of accusation.

"Well, uh..." the marshall began to fidget, the shotgun now seeming an embarrassment to him. He leaned it against the barn door. "You see..."

"Never mind!" Tap cut in. "Get someone to tend these wounded men and someone else to bury the others. We're heading back to the fort. I expect Colonel Bruster will be sending a delegation out after these guns soon. I were you, I'd make damn sure they don't go anywhere."

Shipley nodded in compliance and Tap went into the barn, skirting around the wagon. Against a wall was an old desk and Tap rummaged through the drawers and then attacked the pigeon holes. In one he found an official looking sheaf of papers and he stuck them in a pocket and went outside. Shipley was still there, looking much subdued.

"Slater was a wealthy man, near as I can tell," Tap said to the marshall. "Before the buzzards move in and pick his carcass clean, you'd better make sure Ab Miller gets enough to set him right and give him a stake to boot. Understand?"

Shipley nodded his head again. He didn't feel like giving anyone an argument, especially if it looked like he might get off the hook.

"Good!" Tap said. "You're going to end up making a fine town marshall yet."

Shipley moved off and Tap went into the barn, got a lamp, and took it into Shipley's office. Once there he laid out the papers he'd found in the desk. As he looked them over, Tap felt the heat rise in his face. One of them was signed at the bottom by Colonel Bruster--a recent set of orders outlining the area that was to be covered by Fort McPherson patrols that week. Someone at the fort had to be involved with the gunrunning!

16

Colonel Bruster bustled down the hall holding a lamp with one hand and his robe closed with the other. The front door rattled again and he called out, "I'm coming! I'm coming!" though his last words were stifled by a yawn. He threw open the door to find Tap standing there. "Duncan!" he said in surprise. "Do you know what time it is? It's after one o'clock!" His eyes narrowed down. "You'd better have a good reason for going off and leaving the command..."

Tap raised his hand and stopped him. "Two of them. One about Slater, the other, Wolf Whistle."

"All right! All right! Come in." The colonel padded into the parlor, his slippers making a muffled slapping sound across the wooden floor, and put down the lamp he'd been carrying. Bruster's head came up suddenly and he wrinkled his nose. "My God, man! You smell like a distillery!"

"More like a brewery. Long story. I'll get me to the laundress' shack after. See if there isn't a little warm water left so I can wash some of this off."

Bruster lit another lamp and then got out two large tumblers. "If I'm going to continue being awakened in the middle of the night on your behalf," he grumbled, "I think I'll just give you quarters in my parlor here."

He handed a half-full glass of whisky to Tap--who had placed an Afghan over a chair so he wouldn't get dried flour all over it--and took a seat on a couch opposite the scout. Before either man could speak, a door off the hall opened and Matty came out, her hair flowing loose and long. Tap twisted around in his chair. His heart skipped a beat at the beauty of her in the soft lamplight. He wondered how he could have waited all these years to see her again.

"What is it father...?" Matty began.

"Army business, my dear. No need for you to..."

"I've been in the army as long as you have," she said with a firmness that brooked no debate. "I can listen."

Bruster sighed, took a swallow of his whisky and nodded at

Tap. "So?"

"After I left Hawthorne, I rode to where I figured Wolf Whistle had moved his camp. He was there but Buffalo Lance wasn't. It was Buffalo Lance who led that raid on Grimes...along with, I'm betting, Crazy Horse."

"Crazy Horse!" Bruster almost spit out a mouthful of whisky. "He's Oglala Sioux! What are they...?"

"Buffalo Lance asked his warriors to come. He's still stewing over that raid Hawthorne made. It was his son who was killed..."

"Yes! Yes! I know all that!" Bruster was sitting on the edge of the couch. "Are they planning an attack on the fort?"

"Don't know. Doubt it. Without the rest of the warriors in Wolf Whistle's camp, along with some other Teton bands, he doesn't have enough braves to do much more than hit small patrols..." Tap waved his glass in the air. "Unless he can sucker a command into something like Hawthorne and Grimes ran into."

"Anyway, Wolf Whistle wants a peace parley. I've got one set up for tomorrow. At a place not too far from here." He sat back in his chair. "I know I stuck my neck out pretty far, but I said you'd be there..."

"Do you think it will do any good?"

Tap raised his glass, as if in a toast. "It will if both sides will give a little ground. Wolf Whistle and his other chiefs don't want war. Neither do any of the other bands hunting near here right now...I think."

Matty noticed Tap's glass was empty. She got up, took the bottle from the desk, then walked over and filled his glass. Next she took it from his hand and downed a fair sized portion, neat.

"Matty! What are you doing, girl?"

"Oh, father!" She turned and sat again. "I know what whisky tastes like."

Bruster's face was red and he looked almost apoplectic. "If I don't live to make my star, it won't be an Indian arrow that downs me!" He gave his daughter a withering stare--that she entirely ignored. "It'll be a certain young woman..."

Tap broke in. "If you can promise the Sioux that you'll keep

126

your soldiers from hitting the camps and hunting parties, I think they'll be willing to muzzle Buffalo Lance and ask Crazy Horse to head back to Montana Territory." Tap killed off the rest of his drink. "Taking along some coffee and sugar--peace offerings-- wouldn't hurt, either."

Bruster was quiet for several minutes, rolling over in his mind what Tap had told him. Finally he said, "All right. When you leave, wake up Sergeant Briggs. Have him call out the companies at six..."

"Uh, one thing..." Tap said hesitantly. "Wolf Whistle's coming with just his chiefs. I said you'd do the same. Show with a small escort I mean."

"Very well. I'll only take along a detail of six or seven men from 'C' Company. Now," his voice expressed concern again. "What's this about Mister Slater?"

"Well, he was running guns to the tribes, all right. Caught him with two wagon loads in Demerest."

"Splendid! Did you get Marshall Shipley to help you detain him?"

"Uh, Shipley wasn't about at the time," Tap said, evasively. "Slater and some of his men kinda put up an argument..." He let it drop.

The colonel wasn't exactly a stranger to Tap's ways. "Can I assume that Mister Slater will not be running more guns into the territory..?"

Tap rolled his tongue around his cheek. "No, nor anywhere else, this side a Hades."

Matty caught the inference. "Was there a fight? Are you...?"

Tap held up a hand. "I'm Fine! So's Whittiker. Any problem we have now, that peace meeting can take care of, we have a mind to bend a bit."

Tap and the colonel cleared up a few other details and then Bruster shuffled off to his room. He left Matty--at her insistence and over his admonition about how-unseemly-it-was-at-this - hour-but-what-can-you-do-with-a-daughter-like-that?--to see Tap to the door.

Tap started out then stopped, wanting to linger, despite how frowy he felt with the mixture of beer and dried flour on him. "You certainly know how to dress to impress the young ladies,"

Matty chided him, wrinkling her nose.

"Proper young ladies ain't up at this hour in their bedclothes and alone with gentlemen on their front stoops, either," Tap retorted.

"So? Since when have you been a gentleman? Gentlemen don't make their ladies wait eleven years until their intentions are made known." She stood tip-toed and gave him a quick kiss on the lips. "And what ARE your intentions, Scout Duncan?"

Tap grabbed Matty and swept her up off her feet, crushing her mouth with his. Her arms flailed at her side as he held her in a bear-hug embrace. Then he set her back down, both of them breathless. Matty had a confused look on her face and Tap noted that it was the first time he'd seen her with nothing to say.

"That's what I want to do!" he said, stepping out into a darker part of the porch. "But what my intentions are, I ain't sure, yet. This is still your world," he swept a hand in the direction of the parlor, "and I can't match it for you." He stepped off the porch and into the darkness, heading for the laundry shack.

It would take about three hours to reach Old Buffalo Bull Meadow. Colonel Bruster had a small column of troopers drawn up and mounted on the parade ground at eight-thirty that next morning...along with all of Company 'D.' Nearby the regimental band was playing and when Tap rode Jericho into the area the horse started to jump and crow-hop around. It took a good minute for Tap to settle him down, mainly by making the horse chase his tail in a circle until he got it out of his system.

"Ought'a had saddled Joshua fer todays outin'" Whittiker said, sitting nearby on the headquarters building porch. "Give ya a lot less sass."

"Yeah. But he's still walking a little stiff after the trip to Stanholp. Jericho will have to do." Tap pointed toward 'D' Company. "What's that about?" he said, his voice betraying more than casual interest. "Supposed to be just a detail going."

"Goin' out to scout around," Whittiker said, "lookin' fer Buffalo Lance...and maybe Crazy Horse, he still with him.

128

Make sure they don't get to no mischief whilst you and the Colonel are peacifyin.'"

Whittiker tilted his head toward the captain. "Hawthorne's idee. Bill Forsyth scoutin.'" He stuck a thumb out to indicate the fort's other white scout, standing near the flagpole. The old man spat into the dirt as his comment on the scheme and Tap kicked his horse over to where Bruster sat in his little one-horse buggy. The colonel was busy talking with several of his officers--Hawthorne included--sitting their mounts near the now quiet band.

"Tap! Ready m'boy?" Bruster said as his officers moved off to their commands--except Hawthrone who held his horse in check.

"Yes Colonel, but..." Tap waved toward 'D' Company. "Think we need them out? Not likely any trouble, Wolf Whistle and you come to an agreement. We got troopers about, stirring things up, hostiles might start something."

"On the contrary," Scout Duncan," Hawthorne put in. "By having a force in the field, the hostiles will think twice about starting trouble. We'll be in too good a position to get right after them."

Hawthorne turned back to Colonel Bruster. "Really, Sir. I wish you'd let me bring 'D' Company along with you...out of sight but near." The concern in Hawthorne's voice sounded sincere but Tap wondered if it wasn't just a desire to get near some Indians he could fight. "Remember what happened to General Canby at a peace meeting in California two years ago..." Hawthorne's words trailed off.

Bruster looked at Tap. "That's a valid point, Tap. Canby was shot down while in the middle of negotiating a peace treaty with the Modocs. How trustworthy are these people?"

Tap pushed his hat back, annoyed that Hawthorne had to bring this up now. "Can't speak for the Modocs, Colonel. Guess they had their reasons for doing what they did. Probably nothing a white man would understand, though." Tap looked directly at Hawthorne while his words went to Bruster. "But I know Wolf Whistle. I'd stake my life on his word...and I have, before. He won't be the one to betray this meeting."

Hawthorne flushed and swung his horse around, moving it over next to Sergeant Quinn and Company 'D.' Bruster shook his head. He needed the skills of both these men. If they could learn to get along it would make his job so much easier. As it was, the animosity between them was thick enough to cut with a knife.

Bruster turned and gave a signal to a sergeant who was heading up the column of eight men and several pack mules loaded with gifts. "Let's move out, Sergeant," he said.

At the same time Hawthorne started his command off, the band, arrayed in front of the headquarters building, struck up a two-step, sending Jericho into a short frenzy of hoof-stamping before Tap could line him out.

"Colonel," he called to the buggy after they had cleared the post gate, "Head south-west. I'll catch up in a few minutes." Then Tap rode back over the parade ground to Whittiker, still sitting on the porch. He squinted one eye up at Tap, a question unasked on his face.

"What you got planned for the rest of the day?" Tap queried.

"Well, Hawthorne's got all the scouts he needs. Colonel's got you. Figger I might go down to the laundry house and see if'n I can't give one a the laundresses a squeeze 'er two."

Tap shifted in the saddle, leaning down so his words could be heard over the band, still pounding out a military two-step. "How about doing me a favor?"

"How such?"

"I don't trust Hawthorne to just 'scout around.' Someone here at McPherson's been feeding information to Slater. That's how he was dodging all our patrols. Same person was letting the tribes know where to meet and get the guns."

Whittiker stood, moving next to Jericho. "Who be it?"

"Not sure. Whoever it is, I'm betting they were working both sides of the table. Now and again, they'd pass on to an officer where they 'thought' a band of 'hostiles' would be. That," Tap's words were hard, "is probably how Hawthorne managed to hit the hide-dryers from Wolf Whistle's camp. I wouldn't be surprised, Slater was encouraging that sort of thing

130

just to drum up business for the guns."

Tap sat up straight again, pulling the horse around. "Anyway, be obliged you grabbed a horse and trailed 'D' Company a piece. It keeps to the north, come on back and give the laundress a pinch for me, too. But if it heads south-west, toward the Heart, where Wolf Whistle's band is..." Tap's tone became cold again. "Come on the run for the parley at Old Buffalo Meadow."

Tap caught up with Bruster's buggy and the two rode along in silence for a while. Tap was just about to speak when a horse and rider came charging out of a small grove of cottonwoods on their left. It was Matty.

"What in thunder...!" Bruster said, hauling the buggy to a stop and standing up. Matty was riding astride, in a split, chocolate-brown riding skirt with a matching jacket. On her head was an enlisted man's kepi. When she pulled to a stop the colonel looked like he was going to explode. "MATTY! What do you think...?" What are you doing...?" Finally he spluttered, "WHERE DID YOU GET THAT OUTFIT?" "You're riding like a man..."

"Oh, father! I've seen lots of women ride astride..."

"Martha Canary, maybe but my daughter is no Calamity Jane! Now get back...!"

"Father! I'm going along. It's just a peace meeting and I've never seen wild Indians before..."

"No! It's too dangerous!"

"I stood with you on the parapets when they bombarded Petersburg..."

"Yes! And took ten years off my life when a mortar round landed not thirty feet away!"

"But there's no danger. Tap will be there. You'll be there..."

"Absolutely not!" Bruster said, his face beet red. He turned to his small detail. Corporal Higgins! Please escort Miss..."

"Oh, poo!" Matty said, swinging her horse around. "I'll go back! But I'm going to hate you forever!" She spurred the horse hard and it responded by making a great leap forward on its hind legs before galloping off toward the fort.

131

Bruster sat back down, removed the straw hat he wore and mopped his head with a large handkerchief. Then he ordered the column forward. "By Godfrey!" he muttered. "I look forward to the day when one of you young hotheads take that girl off my hands!"

It was almost noon when Bruster, Tap and the detail arrived at Old Buffalo Meadow. Wolf Whistle and his council were already there, seated on buffalo robes in the lush, green grass of the meadow. The corporal set up a folding camp chair in front of the assembled warriors and the colonel took it, bowing in respect to the tribesmen before he sat. Wolf Whistle and his council watched intently while a soldier unpacked the gifts. He placed them on the blankets spread out in front of the Sioux and several of them went right to the sugar sacks, wetting their fingers with their mouths and then dipping them into the sweet white granules.

While the gifts were being accepted, Tap translated small talk back and forth between the Sioux and the colonel, but once the gifts had been gone through and a pipe passed around, the talk turned serious.

"I know my heart feels the same as all 'The People,'" Wolf Whistle said, speaking of the other Teton bands. He spoke slowly, both because of the solemnity of the occasion and to allow Tap time for translation. "But I can speak only for my village. Still, if my words are good to you, then I believe the other villages will do as I do. We can have peace."

Wolf Whistle took a long draught on his pipe, then went on, his eyes seemingly focused on a time far distant. "Once, long ago, in my grandfather's time, 'The People' lived far to the east. In the land of the tall trees. We walked as free men in those days. We went wherever we wished. Then," he pointed at the soldiers, sitting in a small group behind the colonel, "the white men came. They said the land was theirs. They said we had to go. So, we moved out to the land we live on today." The old chief's face saddened. "Now you say we cannot have even that. You say we cannot roam about. To hunt. To steal horses from our old enemies such as the Crow. To be warriors."

Wolf Whistle was quiet for a time, as if lost in reflection, the age-lines in his face appearing to crease even deeper. Then he shook off his revery, looked up and Tap began to translate his words again. "The white man believes the land should be broken up and small pieces given to each man. We believe it can only be owned by all--to be used by all, its spirit to be shared by all--not broken into parts, its spirit bound in by shiny ropes, trapped." He made a sign with his left fist, then held both wrists crossed in front of his chest, hands closed, the right over the left, the sign for 'imprison.'

"The white man says he will give us some land that we can live on as before while he takes the rest...the best land." The old man studied the ground for a few moments and then looked at Bruster. "I do not like this...but I understand it. The white man is many. We are few. It is now his day. He has the power... as once we did. It is too bad he does not feel the spirit of the land in him, though he tries to catch it with his shiny ropes and wooden lodges."

"So," the old chief sighed, "we will do as he wants...if he treats us with respect and is true to the words on the papers we signed in the past. I will tell Crazy Horse to return to his hunting grounds. I will tell Buffalo Lance he must stay on the path of peace if he wishes to sit in council with me." The old chief sat back and took his pipe up again. He had had his say.

Now Bruster leaned forward and Tap translated to the Sioux. "I am not the Great Chief in Washington." Bruster said. "I am only a little chief. But if I tell him of your words, of the sorrow you feel in your heart over what some of your young men did, I think he will understand. You lost people when the soldiers came and that angered you. Now we both must empty our hearts of the anger." Bruster looked deep into the chief's eyes, both as he spoke and while Tap translated his words. He was probably ten years older than Wolf Whistle but he felt that the man across from him was, in many ways, older and wiser.

Bruster moved his gaze to Tap. He hoped all this was getting through the way he said it, given the difference between the two languages.

"I will try to see that the supplies promised are given you," Bruster went on as Tap continued to translate. "That the lands

133

you live on are not taken by white men seeking the crazy metal or white men wanting the land for themselves."

Now Bruster too was done speaking. He looked at Tap and wondered what effect his words, filtered through the scout, would have. He knew he had little control over either promised rations or land hungry settlers. That was policy set in Washington and often changed by a whim...or the application of money and influence.

Wolf Whistle and his council talked among themselves for a few minutes--then the chief turned back, speaking in English this time. "We go back to gov'ment land. We hunt here, little time more." He swung an arm to indicate the land around him, "then we go gov'ment land. We keep young men from warpath." Wolf Whistle looked deep into the colonel's eyes. "You keep braves," he pointed to the troopers, "from war on our women, our old ones. We can have peace."

Wolf Whistle turned to his council, talking rapidly to them in their language while Tap moved closer to Colonel Bruster. "I think that's it, Colonel. You got yourself a peace." His voice didn't sound overly optimistic. "How long it's good for? Well, depends on the Indian agents not shorting the rations or slipping them flour laced with sawdust...and you keeping the miners out of the land they were given."

Bruster heaved a sigh. "Yes, not an easy task at all. Still, we may have purchased another season of peace. Next year is an election year. Maybe with Grant out of there...who knows?" He shrugged. "Maybe we can get a decent Indian policy formulated...give the tribes honest rations...halt the illegal sale of guns and liquor..."

That reminded Tap of something and he spoke to Horse Catcher, sitting just to Wolf Whistle's left. "My brother. Who was it that told you where to meet to get the many-shoots?"

The warrior thought about it for a moment, rubbing his chin, as if unsure whether to say anything. Then, as if it no longer mattered, he shrugged. "A man came to our camp, once. A soldier. He spoke to Little Elk. After that, Little Elk went to him for word of where we were to meet."

"Can I speak to Little Elk? Is he at your camp?"

"No," the man said, sadly. "He was killed yesterday. In the fight with Two-Bars."

Tap thought back to the Indian Hawthorne had killed...the man Tap had recognized as hanging around the fort and from his stay at the camp. Could that have been Little Elk? "Did Little Elk have a name for this man? The one who came to him?"

"Yes. He called him 'Yellow Arm.'"

Tap's attention was broken away by a shout. "Look!" one of Wolf Whistle's sub-chiefs cried out in English, pointing north, to the hill that swept up behind them. "Snow-On-His-Face!"

"Whittiker?" Tap said, a sinking feeling hitting him.

"There's someone with him," Bruster said as a second horse crested the hilltop and followed Whittiker down.

"Yes!" said Tap, now even more concerned. "Matty!"

17

Whittiker, with Matty close behind, skidded to a stop in front of Bruster and the chiefs. The old scout's face was hard-set but, at first, the Sioux didn't notice, calling out greetings.

"Snow-On-His-Face! It has been a long time, brother!" said one warrior.

"Old White Whiskers! You scared us with your shooting at our camp that night," cried another.

But it wasn't just the Indians who had something to say.

"Matty!" the colonel fumed. "What in the name of..!"

Tap joined in too. "Whit! What happened? Where's Hawthorne..?"

"Shet up, ever'body! I ain't got but one mouth-hole!" Whittiker said, waving his arms in the air.

He nodded to the chiefs, that he recognized their greetings, but turned to Tap. "You was right! Hawthorne headed out east but turned due south after 'bout a half-hour." He spat a stream of juice off to one side. "Headin' straight fer the Heart."

Bruster looked at Tap. "What...?"

"Took the liberty of having Whit track 'D' Company, Colonel. The Captain is heading right for Wolf Whistle's camp on the Heart River."

Though in English, Tap's words were understood by the chiefs who immediately began to chatter among themselves, gathering up their gear as they did. Bruster looked confused. "How could Captain Hawthorne know where their camp is? And what is my daughter doing here, Scout Whittiker?"

"Found her back a piece. Said she was trackin' you. Way she was goin,' would'a ended up in Denver."

"You should have sent her home!" the colonel said, but Whittiker shook his head.

"What with Buffalo Lance an' Crazy Horse havin' braves runnin' 'round the countryside, didn't seem a reason'ble thing to do."

"As for Hawthorne, Colonel," Tap broke in. "Someone at the fort was working with Slater. Telling him where the patrols would be so he could steer clear of them." Tap was talking fast, now. They needed to take action quick if a real war was to be avoided. "I'm betting the same person has been passing on information to some of the officers--or is an officer himself. He's been letting them know where they might find some 'hostiles.'" Tap took Jericho's reins from a trooper. "We mean to keep a peace, we better rattle hocks."

"All right!" Bruster said, and turned to the chiefs. "Wolf Whistle! This was not my plan. I have an officer with a 'bad heart.' Like Buffalo Lance, he only wants to fight."

The Sioux had packed up and mounted their ponies. "What you do?" said Wolf Whistle.

"I'll ride to your camp. I'll stop my 'bad heart.'" Bruster turned to Tap, who was mounting up, as were most of the soldiers. "Can we get there before 'D' company?"

Tap looked at Whittiker. "Whit?"

"Mebbe. They're closer but they got some rough ground to cover. We push, 'bout be a dead heat."

The colonel slapped his palm with a of pair gauntlets, a decision made. "All right! Matty? You get in the buggy. I want to be able to keep an eye on you." He turned to a trooper still dismounted. "Private! Tie her horse to the back of the buggy."

The Indians, followed by the troopers, scouts and Bruster's buggy, headed west, at a canter, toward the Indian camp on the Heart River. The trooper's horses were bigger and stronger but the Indian mounts were tougher so by the time they neared the camp, they were pretty much together.

The camp was set in a shallow depression, ringed on three sides by slightly higher ground. To the far left of the camp the land flattened to a meandering thread of willows and cottonwoods that delineated the wanderings of the Heart River. The camp was laid out in the normal Sioux fashion--lodges, openings to the east--in a large circle.

The horse herd grazed on the fresh grass, above the camp and to the far right, just below the rim of the low hills. The camp itself reposed in blissful unawareness--dogs yapping, children running about stirring up dust, women working at their cookfires or gathering food along the banks of the stream.

The small band of warriors, soldiers and the two scouts--and the colonel and Matty in the buggy--topped a rise at about the same time to look down into the peaceful village. It was still almost two miles away but seemed much closer in the clear air. Tap was just about to exult upon finding the village safe when, on the ridge above the horse herd, another line of riders appeared.

"Look!" Horse Catcher said, and as the little knot of riders watched, two lines of troopers shook out along the rim of the ridge and then started down. The sound of a bugle signaling the staccato bursts of 'charge' drifted through the warm air.

"No!" Colonel Bruster shouted and brought the whip down, hard, across his horse's back. The animal broke into a run, jerking the buggy forward. Matty was thrown to one side on the seat. She grabbed a top support as the little vehicle lurched and bounced down the slope toward the charging troopers. The colonel was immediately followed by the Indians who started whooping and yipping.

The group matched the speed of the soldiers galloping toward the village. By the time they'd covered a half mile the warriors in camp had noticed the charging soldiers and ran out, starting up a sporadic fire. At this distance the light 'popping' of the rifles sounded remote and detached to Tap, but he knew that a mile away men had started dying.

The colonel drew his sidearm and fired it in the air to attract attention, oblivious to the fact he was putting holes in the buggy top. Matty used a hand to cover one ear and gripped the support with the other to keep from being thrown out. Tap also fired his pistol in the air--and was joined by several of Wolf Whistle's council--hoping to attract the attention of both sides, now coming in to close contact on the grassy plain before the camp.

Though Tap was still a mile distance from the fighting, something directly ahead caught his attention. Another line of mounted men was just topping the ridge on the right flank of Hawthorne's charging troopers. It was Buffalo Lance and his warriors. Even at that distance, Tap could make out the bright yellow and black paint that covered Buffalo Lance's face and body. The man paused for only a moment, then led his warriors in a swooping drive down into the flank of the troopers.

Hawthorne, who had been leading the charge at the head of the two lines of troopers, held no men in reserve. This onslaught by an unexpected force drove in his right flank, causing the troopers to drop back, milling, fighting horseman-to-horseman. The warriors who had been left in camp were fewer in number than the attacking troopers but many of them were armed with repeating rifles. They managed to blunt the front of the charge, keeping it from sweeping through the village. Then Hawthorne must have given an order to form a skirmish line because several troopers dismounted to fight on foot as other cavalrymen took up reins and moved the horses to the rear.

At less than a half mile from the battle scene Bruster's little vehicle still bounced and heaved across the rough ground like some sort of mechanical jackrabbit. The buggy, now spied by combatants on both sides, caused the firing to slacken. When the little knot of men with the colonel--his buggy exploding into the air with every hummock and depression it hit--neared the battleground in front of the camp, the fighting drifted to a stop...except in one area.

Toward the end of the ragged fighting line, farthest from the approaching buggy and its followers, several mounted men still fought, wheeling and charging--and two of them were Buffalo Lance and Captain Hawthorne.

The pair continued to spar and feint, even as the others stopped their fighting and watched. Hawthorne wielded a saber, Buffalo Lance a spear. The captain's horse, lathered and tiring, stumbled as it skirted around the Indian pony, which scampered out of the way when Hawthorne tried to strike a blow.

Suddenly Buffalo Lance charged the captain and the winded cavalry horse, pulling up short a dozen or so yards away to luanch the spear at Hawthorne. Hawthorne twisted about in his saddle and deflected it with his saber. Then, with a victorious yell the captain spurred full tilt at the apparently defenseless Sioux warrior. Buffalo Lance also put heel to horse, charging foreward. Just as the two were about to meet, Buffalo Lance slipped off to hang on one side of his horse.

140

The animals, on a dead run, passed each other, Hawthorne's sword stroke flashing above the Indian pony, meeting nothing but air. Buffalo Lance immediately righted himself on his horse, wheeled about and charged back, before Hawthorne could manage to turn his own mount. The warrior swung high a battle-ax that had been looped about the pommel of his war saddle. A few bounds of the Indian pony and the ax was buried in Hawthorne's back. The blow sent the captain reeling out of the saddle as Wolf Whistle, Tap, Bruster and the others thundered up.

"Enough!" Horse Catcher cried, raising his hand and putting his horse across the path of Buffalo Lance. "There will be no more fighting this day!"

Buffalo Lance, the war fury still on him, danced his horse about for a few seconds. He looked around and, seeing the strange congregation of tribesmen and troopers now mingling peacefully, moved off. His face was still battle-set and he rode across where men had just fought, toward a small knot of his warriors standing easy but ready on the far side of the camp.

Bruster dismounted from the buggy, looking over the now-silent battleground. Here and there figures in the grass were still but most warriors--in blue or breechclout--walked or rode about, though not a few nursed wounds. A lieutenant, not completely sure the fighting was over, decided for himself and set some men to tending the injured. The rest of Bruster's officers gathered around him, close by the fallen captain, as did a few of the men from the village.

"Wolf Whistle!" Bruster said, facing the chief and his still-mounted retinue. "I am sorry for this." He swept his hand across the battleground. "I have bad hearts among my people, too."

Bruster turned and walked the few feet to where Captain Hawthorne had pushed himself up on one arm. The other hung useless. Tap took a certain amount of satisfaction in noting that the officer had taken the hatchet in about the same place as the arrow had found him--the upper left shoulder. The hatchet had fallen out and lay nearby.

"Captain!" Bruster barked. "Who gave you the order to

charge this village?"

Hawthorne grimaced, his wound painful but not mortal. "It was a hostile village. Once off the reservation they are open to attack at any time..."

"Not against my direct order," Bruster barked. "You knew I was on my way to a peace meeting." The colonel's face was getting red again. "Such an act could only put that meeting--and, by Godfrey, my life and my daughter's life--in jeopardy!"

He turned to Wolf Whistle again. "Chief. I will do my utmost to see that this man is charged and brought to a court's martial." Bruster noticed the puzzlement on Wolf Whistle's face and turned to Tap. "Could you translate that, m'boy?"

Tap relayed the colonel's words, dubious over whether an ambitious and daring act such as Hawthorne's would ever be censured by the hero-worshipers in the east. At best, he might be reassigned to another fort. Still, he translated. Then he was reminded of something.

"Recognize this, Captain?" Tap said, handing the man the paper he had found in Slater's desk.

Gritting his teeth, Hawthorne shifted to his knees, taking the paper with his right hand. He studied it for a moment and then started to hand it back. It was intercepted by Bruster who could see it was official fort business. "Of course I recognize it," the captain said. "It's a set of orders for last week's patrols. That's my initial at the bottom."

Tap looked over Bruster's shoulder at the scrawl in one corner. He'd wondered what it was and could now make out the stylized 'H.' "You gave this to Slater?" Tap said, disbelief in his voice. He knew Hawthorne to be an insufferable, glory-hunting opportunist, but he had never before doubted that the man was loyal to his profession.

The captain made a face. "Of course not! I gave it to Sergeant Quinn. As I always do with my orders after I've memorized them!"

Tap swiveled around, to where Quinn, listening intently to the conversation, sat his horse. The two men locked eyes and the sergeant immediately realized that he had been exposed. The sergeant pulled his horse around and threw the spurs to it, sending the animal across the battle area, scattering men and horses in his wake.

Tap, galvanized into action, yelled at Jericho who charged forward, letting Tap make a pony-express mount into the saddle. Both men dashed toward the rim of the hill, in the general direction of Demerest, Jericho gaining at every leap...but not for long.

Ahead, point down in the grass, was a battle lance, festooned along one edge with feathers. It was used more as a decoration or war totem than a weapon and it had been dropped by one of Buffalo Lance's men. A light prairie wind now kicked up and blew the feathers upright on the shaft, causing them to seemingly spring from the grass...and Jericho became unglued. The horse pitched and plunged, sending Tap, not expecting anything of this sort, off and into the grass, his rifle gone.

A hundred feet ahead, Sergeant Quinn himself pulled to a stop. Ahead of him there had appeared a line of mounted warriors--Buffalo Lance in the forefront. The war chief had watched Quinn's dash, and, though not fully understanding what was going on, instinctively realized that this man was no friend of the Sioux or the whites.

Quinn whirled his horse around to see Tap, on his feet, trying to catch his horse--without much success. Then the hate washed over the sergeant. Twenty-eight years in the army, from the war with Mexico to now, twenty-eight long, hard years. And, until Slater had offered him money for information, he had nothing to show for it but the stripes on his sleeve and a small room to himself in the barracks. And now it was all lost and it was the scout who had exposed him!

Quinn's jaws tightened. His face flushed red and the scar on his cheek was outlined like a streak of lightening across a darkened sky. Any possible escape was now barred and his fate at the hands of either the Indians or the military would be about the same--death. There was but one act left that he could perform as a free man--revenge! He drew his saber and urged his mount toward Tap, who was still on foot and unawares the sergeant had stopped.

Tap chirped to his horse. "Come on, Jericho. Good horse,"

but the animal continued to back, snorting and pawing. "Come on, you stupid...!" Tap was beginning to lose his patience when he heard the pound of hooves. He turned to see Quinn, who he supposed was still traveling hard away, coming at him, his sword raised, ready for a savage downstroke.

Tap ignored Jericho and drew his pistol, cocking and taking careful aim. Quinn, coming fast, was about twenty feet away when Tap dropped the hammer...to hear the hollow click of an empty chamber. He tried to leap out of the way as the blade swooped down. Quinn, missing with the saber, pulled his horse around and immediately spurred the animal hard on one side, causing the horse to swing its hindquarters. The animal caught Tap full along the right side of his body and sent him flying a good fifteen feet through the air.

Tap hit hard, rolled twice and came up onto his knees, stunned, both hands hanging at his sides. He saw--barely-- through tear-smeared eyes, the wavy figure of Sergeant Quinn pull around for another pass. The little sergeant sent his horse into motion again, the saber raised high but turned blade-up, prepared for a downward thrust, right through Tap's immobile form.

Tap was still on his knees and he could sense the pound of the hooves coming at him and hear the slash of the horse parting the long grass. He even felt the heat of the sun beating down-- but he wasn't able to move his own body to save himself. Quinn's horse flew by Tap, so close he was hit in the shoulder by a swinging stirrup. Tap didn't feel the strike of the sword...nor hear the sound of the lance that sliced through the air, striking Quinn only yards before he reached Tap. He did hear the thud of Quinn's body as it hit the ground, skidding to a stop only a few feet away.

Tap managed to push himself up on one leg to see, in the grass ahead of him, Quinn, lying on his back. The man had a Sioux lance protruding from his chest. His mouth opened and closed silently, like a fish out of water, his eyes stared at the sky. Then the fingers, on outstretched arms, slowly relaxed, his eyes half-closed and his head fell sideways. Buffalo Lance's son had been avenged.

The warrior rode over, reaching a hand down to Tap, pulling him to his feet. "I tried to take your life," said Buffalo Lance, solemnly. "Now I have given it back. Can we be brothers again?"

Tap shook his head to clear it, his arm still gripped by the Indian. "We never stopped being brothers," Tap said, tilting his head to look at the mounted man. Then he grinned. "Except, maybe, for a few minutes after you lit that brush afire."

For the first time since his move to Fort McPherson, Tap saw Buffalo Lance smile. "Good!" He dropped Tap's arm and moved off as the buggy, carrying Matty and her father, hove near.

"Tap! Tap! Are you all right?" Then Matty was out of the buggy and by his side, helping to steady him.

Tap put an arm around Matty, burying his head in her hair for a brief moment. "Seems, every time of late we meet, you have to take inventory to make sure I'm still all in one piece."

She pulled away slightly, looking at him. "If we were together, maybe you'd not always be needing a doctor more than you need me."

Something touched Matty in the back just then and she gave a little jump. It was Jericho, nickering lowly and pushing to get near Tap. "Fool horse!" he said. "Almost got me killed!"

Colonel Bruster walked up. "Bad fall, m'boy! Are you fit?"

Tap grimaced, limping as he took a few steps forward, Matty still at his side. "I'll live, get the proper care."

"So. It was Sergeant Quinn? I never suspected..."

"Guess he fell into cahoots with Slater. Man living on twenty-two dollars a month, what someone like Slater could pay, might look to be pretty good money."

Tap looked down at Matty, then at Jericho. A decision apparently resolved in his head, he took the reins of his horse and handed them to the colonel. "From me to you, Colonel. He'll do just fine between a buggy's shafts."

"For me?" The colonel said. "Splendid! But, let me pay you for him..."

"Nope. It's a gift. Sort of a token." Tap glanced at Matty and he could see she understood what he was about. "All I want for him is your blessing...on Matty and me, we get married."

"Married?" Bruster gave a start and Tap looked worried.

"If...that is. if you don't mind..."

"Mind? My boy, you don't know...No! I don't mind! Certainly! Certainly...you have my blessing."

"One, thing, Colonel," Tap said. "Jericho, he's pretty headstrong. Like you saw, he's got a mind of his own and can be as stubborn as a mule."

Bruster peered out from under his bushy eyebrows, looking first at the horse, then to Matty and finally Tap. "My boy, let me tell you something..."

Matty broke in. "Don't say it, father!" Her face was grim. "Not if you ever want to see your grandchildren!"

"Yes, yes, well. Just let me say, Tap, you don't know how happy I am...for both of you..."

"Ho, brothers," Wolf Whistle called out in English, trotting up with Horse Catcher. "Some die. Not many. Some hurt. Soldier and Injun. Not many."

"Good!" Bruster said, his voice hopeful. "Can we keep the peace, Wolf Whistle?"

"We keep. You stop soldier bad hearts. We stop braves. "Mebbe so, we not fight more." He put his hand down and Bruster reached up and took it, both men arm to arm.

"When my soldiers are taken care of, Wolf Whistle," Bruster said. "I'll send our doctor out here--to look at your wounded."

"One other thing," the colonel said, moving back. "Your hunting is almost over. How would you feel about giving up your repeaters? The army changed over from the fifty calibers to the new forty-fives a few years back." Bruster sounded cheerful, trying to put as good a face on his offer as he could. "I might be able to get you some of the fifty's. Fine rifles. Breechloaders, just like the ones we use now..."

Wolf Whistle looked at the '66 Winchester he had in his hand and then at the single-shot Springfield carbine held by a nearby soldier. He shook his head, making a face as he did. "No. We trade much for many-shoots. We keep. Need next year when all Lakota meet to hunt. On Greasy Grass." The chief raised his hand again in a peace gesture and turned toward the

146

camp.

"Oh, well," Bruster said, philosophically. "It was worth a try."

Tap put an arm around Matty again. "Peace. Could be, your new husband will be out of a job," he said, lightheartedly. "Going to be even harder to afford keeping you in your world."

"Doesn't matter," she said, giving him a squeeze. "We'll make our own world."

Tap and Matty walked over to the buggy. "We fit in, Colonel?" Tap asked. "Don't feel much like sitting a saddle just now."

"Hop aboard, my boy!" Bruster said, jovially. "Hop aboard!" As soon as they were seated, with Jericho tied to the back, the colonel clicked the horse ahead. "One thing, Tap," he asked.

"Yes sir?"

"Greasy Grass? Wolf Whistle said the tribes would be gathering there next year. Where in the devil is that?"

"River. Montana Territory. Good hunting ground up around there. And good grass. Big enough for all the bands to gather. Greasy Grass River is their name for it." Tap put his arm around Matty and held her close on the buggy seat. "It's on a tributary of the Yellowstone. Whites call it The Little Big Horn."

END

147

ABOUT THE AUTHOR

The author has had a life-long interest in the Old West and has contributed many historical articles over the years to various Old West magazines. He also writes a monthly column for a local newspaper on the history of California's Gold Rush days.

The author retired ten years ago from a job as an electronic manufacturing manager. Since then he has devoted his time between spoiling his grandchildren, riding his horse in the Sierra Foothills, adding to his antique firearms collection and working on an Old West series featuring the frontier character Tap Duncan. He has also completed several other novels pertaining in one way or the other to the period of the early West.